THE WEALTH
YOU WERE NEVER TAUGHT

WHY SMH AND QQQ HOLD THE KEY TO
FINANCIAL FREEDOM IN A CHANGING WORLD

CHAKIB ABI SAAB

Copyright © 2025 Chakib Abi Saab
All rights reserved.

No part of this book may be reproduced in any form or by any electronic or mechanical means, including photocopying, recording, or any information storage and retrieval system, without the written permission of the publisher, except for the brief quotations in critical reviews or articles.

The Wealth You Were Never Taught

CONTENTS

INTRODUCTION 5

01
THE WEALTH EQUATION THEY NEVER TAUGHT YOU 9

02
TECH IS THE NEW REAL ESTATE 33

03
MEET SMH AND QQQ 61

04
THE PSYCHOLOGY OF WEALTH BUILDING 91

05
BUILDING A BULLETPROOF WEALTH STRATEGY 117

06
WHAT THE MARKET DOESN'T SAY OUT LOUD 143

07
YOUR FREEDOM NUMBER 169

08
THE 3 ENEMIES OF WEALTH 191

09
OWN THE FUTURE 213

CONCLUSION 235

INTRODUCTION
THE NEW RULES OF WEALTH

You do not need to be an expert. You do not need a finance degree. You do not need a lucky break.

You need a clear strategy. A strong mindset. And the willingness to begin.

Because wealth is not about how much you earn. It is about how much you own. And how early you start owning the right things.

SMH and QQQ are not magic. They are not shortcuts. But they are something far more powerful. Predictable long-term vehicles for compounding your capital backed by the most important trend of our generation: technology's exponential rise.

If you have ever felt like the system was rigged like you were playing catch-up or like building wealth was something other people figured out, this book is for you.

And if you have ever felt like your time is worth more, your life could be freer, and your future should feel lighter, then this book is not just for you.

It is your blueprint.

Welcome to The Wealth You Were Never Taught.

Let's begin.

They are investing in the real engines of the future. Technology. Innovation. The digital infrastructure that powers everything from your phone to the global economy. And they are doing it through two of the most powerful financial tools available today: **SMH and QQQ**.

This book, **The Wealth You Were Never Taught**, is not about hype. It is about alignment.

It is the exact framework I have used to build meaningful wealth. Not through luck. Not through perfect timing. But through strategic consistency and a deep understanding of where the world is heading.

I am not a financial influencer. I am not here to sell a dream. I have spent my career leading technology and innovation at a global scale and I built this system for myself long before I ever thought of writing a book about it.

Let me be clear. I would never tell anyone to invest blindly. You should never take financial advice without doing your own due diligence. But I do recommend this.

Take this seriously.

Because what you are about to read can change your life. Not because it promises instant returns. But because it gives you something more important. Control. Clarity. And a system that actually works in the real world.

Look around.

The world is not just changing. It is accelerating. Faster than governments can regulate. Faster than schools can adapt. And certainly faster than traditional financial advice can keep up.

The rules that built wealth fifty years ago are broken. The playbooks your parents followed are obsolete. Even the so-called new gurus shouting on your social feed are mostly noise.

But in the middle of all this chaos, something rare is happening. Clarity.

A small group of people are quietly getting wealthier. Faster. With more confidence than ever before. Not because they found a secret trick or hacked the system. But because they understood where value is moving and positioned themselves to ride that wave.

They are not chasing meme stocks.

They are not glued to financial news or guessing what the Fed will do next.

They are not waiting for permission.

ABOUT THE AUTHOR

Seasoned Excecutive with 20+ yeas of experience in C-level positions in complex multinational environments

Chakib Abi Saab is a seasoned technology executive and strategic investor with over two decades of experience leading innovation across global enterprises. As Chief Technology and Innovation Officer for multinational organizations, he has been at the forefront of deploying transformative technologies that reshape industries and accelerate performance.

Through years of building and scaling digital solutions, Chakib developed a deep understanding of where technology was heading. That perspective gave him a clear sense of where long-term value would emerge in the market and shaped the investment philosophy at the heart of this book.

01

THE WEALTH EQUATION THEY NEVER TAUGHT YOU

WHY TRADITIONAL ADVICE KEEPS
YOU PLAYING SMALL AND WHAT THE
WEALTHY DO DIFFERENTLY

MAIN POINTS

» The Illusion of Security

How the 9–5 and savings-only mindset stunts **financial growth**

» Compound Growth vs. Compounded Regret

The hidden power of early investing

» The Cashflow Trap

Why earning more isn't enough, and how wealth actually works

» Assets, Not Hours

The difference between working for money and owning your time

» Think Like a Capital Allocator

Shift from consumer to investor with one mindset tweak

» The Wealth Gap Is a Knowledge Gap

Why most people never even see the path to financial freedom

THE ILLUSION OF SECURITY

HOW THE NINE TO FIVE AND SAVINGS ONLY MINDSET STUNTS FINANCIAL GROWTH

Security is a story we have been told since childhood. Study hard. Get a good job. Work your way up. Save what you can. Retire someday. The storyline feels safe, familiar, and responsible. But the problem with this script is not that it lacks effort or intention. It is that it was written for a world that no longer exists.

In that world, job loyalty was rewarded. Pensions were standard. Housing prices were reasonable. The pace of change was slow and predictable. And you could park your money in a savings account and still beat inflation. That world gave you a sense that if you stayed within the lines, life would work out.

But that world is gone.

Today, the ground moves faster. Jobs are no longer permanent. They are platforms. Skills have expiration dates. Economic cycles are shorter and sharper. Inflation quietly erodes the value of your money whether you see it or not. What once felt secure now exposes you to a new kind of risk. A quiet, invisible kind. The risk of falling behind while doing everything right.

This is the great irony of modern life. People are working harder than ever. They are staying employed. They are saving diligently. Yet they feel less financially secure year after year. Why does this happen? Because security is not found in hard work alone. Security lives in ownership. Not in the hours you put in, but in the assets you build.

And here lies the trap. Most people confuse stability with safety.

Holding a job feels stable. Having some savings feels responsible. But stability without growth becomes fragility over time. If your financial well-being depends solely on your ability to work and save, then you are one layoff, one illness, or one missed opportunity away from crisis. That is not security. That is exposure.

Real security is not about avoiding risk. It is about choosing the right risks and owning the upside. The wealthy understand this. They do not aim for safety by avoiding volatility. They pursue strategic exposure to assets that appreciate over time. Businesses. Real estate. Intellectual property. And increasingly, technology-powered funds like QQQ and SMH.

They play a different game because they use a different equation.

The average person trades time for money and saves what is left. The wealthy trade money for assets and let those assets work for them. One path is linear. The other is exponential.

And yet, this is not about class or privilege. It is about mindset. Everyone has access to the tools. Everyone has the choice to start. What separates those who build wealth from those who do not is not intelligence. It is orientation. The wealthy orient their lives around ownership, not activity. They know that effort alone has a ceiling. Ownership does not.

Look closely and you will see a quiet revolution already underway. A generation is waking up to the limits of traditional advice. They are not rejecting work. They are rejecting the idea that work alone will get them where they want to go. They are building portfolios, not just careers. They are chasing freedom, not just income.

This is your wake-up call.

If you want real security, stop seeking comfort in the predictable and start building conviction in the exponential. Stop measuring your life in hours and start measuring it in ownership. That shift changes everything.

In the chapters that follow, we will rewire your thinking, reshape your strategy, and reintroduce you to a truth the system never taught you. Wealth is not about playing it safe. It is about playing it smart.

And smart starts now.

COMPOUND GROWTH VERSUS COMPOUNDED REGRET

THE HIDDEN POWER OF EARLY INVESTING

There is a quiet force in the world of wealth that most people underestimate. It does not make headlines. It is not flashy. But it is relentless. It is what turns average decisions into extraordinary outcomes. It rewards patience more than brilliance. And it punishes hesitation more than failure.

That force is compound growth.

Most people hear the term and nod as if they understand it. They have seen the math. They know the charts. But few truly grasp what compounding means at a human level. Compound growth is not just an investing concept. It is a

MAIN POINTS

» The Illusion of Security

How the 9–5 and savings-only mindset stunts **financial growth**

» Compound Growth vs. Compounded Regret

The hidden power of early investing

» The Cashflow Trap

Why earning more isn't enough, and how wealth actually works

» Assets, Not Hours

The difference between working for money and owning your time

» Think Like a Capital Allocator

Shift from consumer to investor with one mindset tweak

» The Wealth Gap Is a Knowledge Gap

Why most people never even see the path to fi-nancial freedom

THE ILLUSION OF SECURITY

HOW THE NINE TO FIVE AND SAVINGS ONLY MINDSET STUNTS FINANCIAL GROWTH

Security is a story we have been told since childhood. Study hard. Get a good job. Work your way up. Save what you can. Retire someday. The storyline feels safe, familiar, and responsible. But the problem with this script is not that it lacks effort or intention. It is that it was written for a world that no longer exists.

In that world, job loyalty was rewarded. Pensions were standard. Housing prices were reasonable. The pace of change was slow and predictable. And you could park your money in a savings account and still beat inflation. That world gave you a sense that if you stayed within the lines, life would work out.

But that world is gone.

Today, the ground moves faster. Jobs are no longer permanent. They are platforms. Skills have expiration dates. Economic cycles are shorter and sharper. Inflation quietly erodes the value of your money whether you see it or not. What once felt secure now exposes you to a new kind of risk. A quiet, invisible kind. The risk of falling behind while doing everything right.

This is the great irony of modern life. People are working harder than ever. They are staying employed. They are saving diligently. Yet they feel less financially secure year after year. Why does this happen? Because security is not found in hard work alone. Security lives in ownership. Not in the hours you put in, but in the assets you build.

And here lies the trap. Most people confuse stability with safety.

Holding a job feels stable. Having some savings feels responsible. But stability without growth becomes fragility over time. If your financial well-being depends solely on your ability to work and save, then you are one layoff, one illness, or one missed opportunity away from crisis. That is not security. That is exposure.

Real security is not about avoiding risk. It is about choosing the right risks and owning the upside. The wealthy understand this. They do not aim for safety by avoiding volatility. They pursue strategic exposure to assets that appreciate over time. Businesses. Real estate. Intellectual property. And increasingly, technology-powered funds like QQQ and SMH.

They play a different game because they use a different equation.

The average person trades time for money and saves what is left. The wealthy trade money for assets and let those assets work for them. One path is linear. The other is exponential.

And yet, this is not about class or privilege. It is about mindset. Everyone has access to the tools. Everyone has the choice to start. What separates those who build wealth from those who do not is not intelligence. It is orientation. The wealthy orient their lives around ownership, not activity. They know that effort alone has a ceiling. Ownership does not.

Look closely and you will see a quiet revolution already underway. A generation is waking up to the limits of traditional advice. They are not rejecting work. They are rejecting the idea that work alone will get them where they want to go. They are building portfolios, not just careers. They are chasing freedom, not just income.

This is your wake-up call.

If you want real security, stop seeking comfort in the predictable and start building conviction in the exponential. Stop measuring your life in hours and start measuring it in ownership. That shift changes everything.

In the chapters that follow, we will rewire your thinking, reshape your strategy, and reintroduce you to a truth the system never taught you. Wealth is not about playing it safe. It is about playing it smart.

And smart starts now.

COMPOUND GROWTH VERSUS COMPOUNDED REGRET

THE HIDDEN POWER OF EARLY INVESTING

There is a quiet force in the world of wealth that most people underestimate. It does not make headlines. It is not flashy. But it is relentless. It is what turns average decisions into extraordinary outcomes. It rewards patience more than brilliance. And it punishes hesitation more than failure.

That force is compound growth.

Most people hear the term and nod as if they understand it. They have seen the math. They know the charts. But few truly grasp what compounding means at a human level. Compound growth is not just an investing concept. It is a life principle. It is the difference between reacting and building. Between dabbling and committing. Between living at the mercy of money and putting money to work for you.

Here is how it works. When you invest money, it grows. But when that growth itself starts to grow, something remarkable happens. Each year, your gains generate their own gains. Over time, the curve bends. It starts to accelerate. What began as a slow climb becomes a steep trajectory. At first it feels like nothing is happening. Then it feels like everything is happening all at once.

The key is not just growth. The key is **early** growth.

This is where most people lose the game before they even begin. They delay. They tell themselves they will start investing once they earn more, once the timing feels right, once they are more confident. But in the world of compounding, time is the multiplier. Delay is the costliest decision of all.

Let us be clear. Every year you wait is not just a year lost. It is a year that robs your future self of exponential return. You are not just losing the growth of that year. You are losing the compound impact of every future year that would have built on it. That is why compounding is so powerful when you start young and so painful when you start late.

Imagine two people. One begins investing at age twenty five, puts in five hundred dollars a month for ten years, and then stops completely. The other waits until age thirty five and starts investing five hundred dollars a month consistently until retirement. Even though the second person invests for three times as long and puts in three times the money, the first person still often ends up with more. Why? Because their money had more time to grow on top of itself. That is the magic of compounding. And it does not wait for you to be ready.

But compound growth has a shadow. A mirror image that works just as relentlessly in the other direction.

It is called compounded regret.

This is what happens when the cost of inaction builds up over time. When you miss out on growth, not because the opportunity was unavailable, but because the decision to start was never made. Regret compounds like debt. Slowly at first. Then all at once. You do not feel it in your twenties. You start noticing it in your thirties. By your forties, it becomes a question you cannot ignore. Why did I not start sooner?

Compounded regret is the tax we pay for hesitation. It shows up not just in your net worth but in your freedom. The trip you could not afford. The risk you could not take. The opportunity you had to decline. Not because you lacked talent or work ethic, but because you lacked capital. The capital that would have been there had you simply started earlier.

The irony is that most people do not need to be convinced to invest. They already believe it is the right thing to do. What they need is urgency. They need to stop thinking about investing as a task and start seeing it as a race against time. Every day you wait, someone else's future is pulling ahead of yours. Not because they are smarter. Because they started.

This is why investing in long-term vehicles like QQQ and SMH matters so much. These are not just high-performance funds. They are compounding machines. They hold companies with durable growth, scalable models, and network effects that multiply over time. When you invest in them consistently and early, you are not betting on luck. You are aligning yourself with the very math that builds empires.

And here is the truth that many people miss. You do not need to invest large amounts. You need to invest consistently. Small contributions grow into large results when given enough time and discipline. Compound growth rewards action. Even imperfect action. But it ignores intentions. It only works if you put your money in motion.

So ask yourself one question. What would your future look like if you gave compound growth the time it needs to do its work? And what will it cost you if you do not?

One leads to freedom. The other leads to regret.

You get to choose which one multiplies.

THE CASHFLOW TRAP

WHY EARNING MORE IS NOT ENOUGH AND HOW WEALTH ACTUALLY WORKS

Everywhere you look, the world tells you to earn more. Hustle harder. Climb higher. Chase the next promotion. Build the next side income stream. The obsession with earning is deep and emotional. It is tied to pride, identity, even survival. And yet, for all the energy poured into chasing income, very few people ever build lasting wealth.

The reason is simple. Earning more is not the same as becoming wealthier.

Most people live in what I call the cashflow trap. It is a mindset and a system that rewards activity but never translates that activity into freedom. It works like this. You work. You get paid. You spend. Maybe you save a little. Then you repeat the cycle next month. The numbers might change, but the structure never does. Your lifestyle expands to match your income. Your obligations increase. Your stress does too. And the illusion of progress keeps you busy while your wealth stays flat.

This is how high income earners can stay broke for decades. They bring in six figures or more, but they own almost nothing that grows without them. They have the car. The house. The nice vacations. But no real assets. No cashflow that continues when they stop working. No equity in the system. Just a higher level of dependence disguised as success.

This trap does not care how smart you are. In fact, the more capable you are, the more dangerous the trap becomes. You get rewarded for your performance. You start believing that performance alone will lead to freedom. But money earned is not the same as money retained. And money retained is not the same as money that multiplies.

To break out of the trap, you need a different model.

Wealth does not come from the amount you earn. It comes from the gap between what you earn and what you reinvest into appreciating assets. The goal is not to have money flow through you. The goal is to have money stay with you, work for you, and eventually move without you.

When you look at truly wealthy individuals, you will find a pattern. They do not just earn well. They convert income into ownership. They own equity in businesses. They own real estate. They own intellectual property. And increasingly, they own shares in growth-oriented funds like QQQ and SMH. These are instruments that do not just preserve capital. They compound it.

This is why owning matters more than earning.

Ownership creates leverage. It separates your time from your income. While the cashflow trap requires you to show up every month to keep the machine running, ownership builds momentum even while you rest. It gives you time. It gives you optionality. It gives you power.

Let me be clear. Earning money is not the problem. You should earn as much as you can. The problem is when earning becomes the ceiling instead of the engine. When all of your financial focus goes into producing income instead of acquiring assets. When every dollar you make is already spoken for before it has a chance to grow.

To escape the cashflow trap, you need to make one critical shift. Treat your income not as your reward, but as your resource. It is the fuel. Not the finish line. Your real financial life begins when you start asking better questions. Not how much did I make this month, but how much did I keep. Not how much did I keep, but how much did I invest. Not how much did I invest, but how much did I own that continued to grow.

This is where QQQ and SMH enter the picture again. These are not just ETFs. They are ecosystems of innovation. QQQ holds some of the most dominant tech companies of our generation. SMH tracks the companies that design and manufacture the chips that power nearly every digital device. Together, they represent ownership in the future economy. Ownership that grows whether you are working or not.

You cannot outrun the cashflow trap by working harder. You break it by building smarter. You shift your identity from earner to owner. From consumer to investor. From worker to architect.

And the best part is that you do not need millions to start. You need intention. You need consistency. And you need the courage to stop measuring success in income and start measuring it in equity.

The trap ends the moment you decide to step off the treadmill and start building your own engine.

ASSETS NOT HOURS

THE DIFFERENCE BETWEEN WORKING FOR MONEY AND OWNING YOUR TIME

Most people spend their entire adult life working for money. They wake up, go to work, give their time and energy, and get a paycheck in return. Then they do it again the next week, the next month, the next year. Decades go by, and the equation never really changes. The idea of financial progress is tied directly to time. The more hours you give, the more income you make. The logic feels sound, but the system is flawed.

You can only work so many hours. You can only take on so many projects. Your energy is finite. Your health is not permanent. Your time is not scalable. And yet, most people continue to tie their financial future to their ability to perform and deliver on demand. This is the mindset that leads to burnout. It also leads to stagnation. Because no matter how skilled or dedicated you are, you are still operating in a world of fixed input and fixed output.

Trading time for money is how you start. It is not how you build wealth.

Wealth lives on the other side of that exchange. It begins when you shift your focus from hours to assets. From income to ownership. From transactions to accumulation. Assets are not bound by time. Assets are not limited by your schedule. Assets are the only vehicle that allow you to separate effort from reward and begin creating real leverage in your life.

This is the first real inflection point for anyone serious about freedom. Not the freedom to take a longer vacation. The freedom to control your time. To say yes to the right things and no to everything else. To step out of survival mode and into strategy. That shift begins the moment you ask yourself one question.

What do I own that will grow without me?

If the answer is nothing, then your financial system is fragile. Because the minute you stop working, everything stops with you. But if you begin to acquire assets, assets that produce income, appreciate in value, or hold equity in growing markets, you begin to build a different kind of life. One with momentum. One with compounding. One with time on your side.

Let us make it practical. When you invest in a fund like QQQ or SMH, you are not just buying stock. You are buying into companies that are building, scaling, and innovating every single day. While you are at your job, they are expanding their margins, growing their user base, launching new products, acquiring competitors. And as a shareholder, you benefit from all of it. You are not trading your time. You are owning their progress.

That is what an asset does. It extends your reach. It multiplies your effort. It builds even while you sleep. It is working for you when you are on vacation, when you are with your family, when you are recovering from burnout, when you are planning your next move. Assets allow you to get paid without showing up. Not because you are doing nothing, but because you did something intelligent long before.

And this is not just about financial gain. It is about the quality of life you are designing. Because when you are no longer trapped in the loop of earning and spending, you begin to experience space. You begin to experience clarity. You begin to think long term. That is where your best decisions come from. Not when you are stressed and stretched thin. But when you are strategic and free to choose.

Most people think freedom comes when they earn more. But earning more still depends on activity. The real shift happens when you start to own more. Because ownership gives you leverage. Leverage gives you control. And control gives you the one resource no job will ever provide at scale. Time.

Ask yourself honestly. What would your life look like if your income no longer depended on your hours? How would you work differently? Live differently? Think differently? That version of you is not just a dream. It is a direct outcome of how you structure your financial life today.

The most powerful thing you can do is stop measuring your value in hours and start multiplying your value through assets. Not someday. Not when the market feels safer. Not after the next raise. Now.

Every share you own, every fund you build, every asset you acquire is a step toward a future where you own your time. Where your calendar reflects your values. Where your income reflects your decisions, not just your effort.

Assets over hours is not a motivational slogan. It is the foundation of financial independence. And once you cross that threshold, you will never look at your time the same way again.

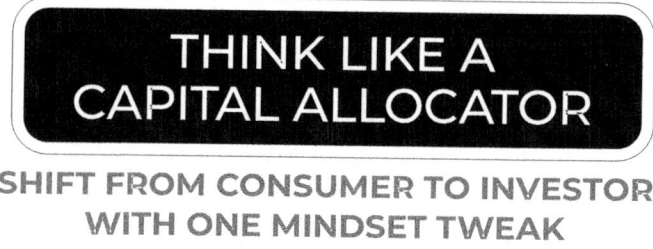

SHIFT FROM CONSUMER TO INVESTOR WITH ONE MINDSET TWEAK

Most people think like consumers. They spend based on how they feel. They earn based on what they are told they are worth. They save what is left and hope it will be enough someday. It is reactive. It is emotional. It is passive. They respond to opportunities instead of designing them. They accumulate things instead of building leverage. This mindset is everywhere because it is easy. It is also expensive.

Wealthy people think differently. They are not obsessed with consumption. They are obsessed with capital. And more specifically, with where to place it. They think like capital allocators.

This is one of the most important mindset shifts you can make. It changes everything about how you approach money, time, energy, and opportunity. When you begin thinking like a capital allocator, you stop asking what you can afford. You start asking what is the best possible use of your resources right now.

Capital allocation is not just a financial skill. It is a worldview. It is the lens through which every decision becomes strategic. You stop treating your paycheck like a reward and start treating it like an opportunity. You stop defaulting to spending and start prioritizing ownership. You ask not just what feels good today but what builds momentum for tomorrow.

Every dollar you earn has a job. It can be consumed. It can be saved. Or it can be invested. The goal is not to eliminate spending. The goal is to maximize return. That return can take many forms. Growth. Income. Freedom. Time. Optionality. Your job as an allocator is to direct your capital toward the options that offer the greatest upside with acceptable risk.

That is what CEOs do. That is what fund managers do. That is what every great investor does. They wake up every day and make decisions about where to place capital. Not based on emotion. Based on conviction. Based on opportunity. Based on long-term thinking.

You can do the same thing. You are not managing billions. But you are managing your future. And the principles are exactly the same.

When you think like a capital allocator, you no longer see investing as something separate from daily life. It becomes the backbone of how you operate. Every financial decision becomes a choice between compounding value and diminishing return. Every hour you spend working is an input into your allocation system. Every purchase you consider becomes a question of alignment. Does this move me toward freedom, or away from it?

Nowhere is this mindset more powerful than in how you build a portfolio. A consumer asks, what is hot right now. What is trending. A capital allocator asks, where is long-term value being created. Who has structural advantages. Who has pricing power. Who is building networks, platforms, and defensible scale. That is why funds like QQQ and SMH are not just smart investments. They are strategic capital allocation plays.

QQQ gives you access to the most innovative, resilient, and well-capitalized technology companies on the planet. These are firms with global reach, elite talent, and dominant market positions. SMH puts you into the core of the semiconductor industry, which powers every modern technology from smartphones to artificial intelligence. You are not guessing. You are allocating. You are placing capital where value is being created and multiplied every single day.

You are also removing friction. When you invest in well-constructed ETFs like QQQ and SMH, you are not just choosing high-quality assets. You are choosing simplicity. You are choosing automation. You are choosing to direct your capital without having to manage every detail. That frees up your mental energy to think about strategy instead of stress. About vision instead of volatility.

And here is the most important part. Thinking like a capital allocator is not about perfection. It is about consistency. You will never have perfect information. You will never time the market exactly right. But if you consistently place your capital where growth and innovation are happening, you will consistently outperform those who wait, react, and guess.

You will also begin to see capital differently. It is not just money. It is attention. It is time. It is relationships. When you start thinking like an allocator, you begin to manage every part of your life through the lens of return. Where should I put my energy this week. Who should I spend time with. What conversations move me forward. What inputs create better outcomes.

This mindset rewires everything. You become less reactive. You become more intentional. You move from scarcity to strategy. From hustle to leverage.

So stop asking what you can afford. Start asking what your capital is doing for you. Start placing it where it matters. Start thinking like an owner, not just an earner.

Capital is not just what you have. It is what you direct. And the moment you begin to allocate it with purpose, you stop playing small.

You start playing to win.

THE WEALTH GAP IS A KNOWLEDGE GAP

WHY MOST PEOPLE NEVER EVEN SEE THE PATH TO FINANCIAL FREEDOM

When we talk about the wealth gap, most people think about income. Some think about opportunity. A few think about privilege. But there is something deeper underneath it all. Something quieter, more persistent, and far more influential than most realize.

The wealth gap is ultimately a knowledge gap.

The difference between those who accumulate wealth and those who struggle to get ahead is not just access to capital. It is access to insight. To perspective. To frameworks that shift behavior before the money even shows up. Wealth is not created in isolation. It is created through decisions. And those decisions are shaped by the knowledge you have, or do not have.

The truth is most people are never taught how money really works. They are taught how to earn, how to spend, maybe how to save. But they are not taught how to allocate. They are not shown how to evaluate risk. They are not given the tools to build a portfolio. They are certainly not introduced to the principles of ownership, compounding, or asymmetric upside. These ideas are rarely found in school. And when they are shared in the real world, they are often buried behind jargon, complexity, or exclusivity.

Meanwhile, the wealthy learn early. Not necessarily in school, but in conversation. In environment. In exposure. They hear different ideas around the dinner table. They see different models of success. They internalize different questions. How do I make my money work for me. Where should I place my capital. What assets will outpace inflation. These are not advanced investment theories. These are basic building blocks. But they are invisible to the people who never receive them.

This is what keeps the gap alive. It is not just inequality of income. It is inequality of information. And information compounds. Just like capital. If you learn something valuable in your twenties and apply it, you benefit for decades. If you miss that insight until your forties or fifties, you spend years playing catch up. Not because you lack ability, but because no one ever showed you the game being played.

And let us be clear. This is not about intelligence. It is about access. You can be brilliant and still build nothing if no one ever hands you the map. You can be highly educated and still financially lost if your education did not include real financial literacy. That is not your fault. But it becomes your responsibility the moment you see it clearly.

The good news is that once you recognize the knowledge gap, you can close it. You can change the trajectory of your life with insight. You do not need a hundred thousand dollars to start building wealth. You need the right questions, the right principles, and the right strategy. That is why this book exists. To give you the map that most people never receive. To show you what is possible when you align your thinking with the mechanics of real wealth.

Start with this simple truth. Wealth is not random. It is not reserved. It is built. And it is built by people who understand how the system actually works. People who know that markets are not chaos. They are compounding machines. People who know that opportunity is not about timing the perfect day. It is about consistently investing in the right places over time. People who know that ETFs like QQQ and SMH are not just stock tickers. They are access points to the most powerful economic engines in the modern world.

These people are not guessing. They are not gambling. They are allocating based on knowledge. They are executing based on conviction. They are winning because they were willing to learn the rules and apply them consistently.

You can do the same.

You do not need permission. You do not need perfection. You need clarity. You need direction. And you need action.

Close the knowledge gap, and you will close the wealth gap. Not overnight, but inevitably. Because once you understand how wealth is created, you can stop hoping for it and start building it.

And when you build it from knowledge, it lasts.

02
TECH IS THE NEW REAL ESTATE

WHY THE MODERN ECONOMY
REWARDS CHIPS AND INNOVATION,
NOT BRICKS AND MORTAR

MAIN POINTS

» **From Steel to Silicon**
The evolution of economic engines and where value lives now

» **The Rise of Digital Infrastructure**
Why semiconductors (SMH) are the backbone of everything

» **Software Eats the World**
QQQ's dominance in tech, biotech, and platform businesses

» **Legacy Assets vs. Living Assets**
Why some investments age like wine and others like milk

» **The Innovation Flywheel**
How tech accelerates its own value and drives market momentum

» **Why Parking Money in the Past Is Riskier Than the Future**
A wake-up call for traditional investors

FROM STEEL TO SILICON

THE EVOLUTION OF ECONOMIC ENGINES AND WHERE VALUE LIVES NOW

Every generation has a story about where wealth comes from. In one era, it was land. Whoever owned the most territory held the power. In the next, it was factories. The industrialist with the most steel and the longest rail lines won the game. Later, it was oil. Energy production became the currency of global influence. For the past century, real estate became the default path to prosperity. Buy property. Hold it. Let time do the rest. It worked well for a while. It created stability. It created equity. It became the dream.

But today, the source of wealth has moved again. It no longer lives in land, or steel, or oil. It lives in silicon. In code. In innovation. In the invisible infrastructure that powers your phone, your car, your business, and your entire life. Wealth has migrated. And the people who understand that shift are building fortunes. The people who do not are watching their strategies lose relevance year by year.

We are living through the largest reallocation of value in human history. Value is moving away from physical assets and toward digital engines. The world's most valuable companies no longer manufacture things. They design networks. They own data. They scale platforms that operate in the cloud, deliver globally, and monetize intelligence instead of inventory.

Amazon does not own shelves. It owns logistics algorithms. Apple does not just sell phones. It owns an ecosystem of devices, software, and recurring revenue. NVIDIA does not sell finished products to consumers. It sells the processing power that fuels artificial intelligence.

This is the economy of silicon. Not just the physical chips but the mental models that dominate scale. Faster iteration. Global distribution. Asymmetric margins. These are not fringe trends. They are foundational truths of modern capitalism.

You do not need to be an engineer to see it. Just look at the stock market. The companies that make up the majority of the Nasdaq have dramatically outperformed almost every traditional sector over the last two decades. They are not riding temporary waves. They are building structural advantages. They attract capital, talent, and intellectual property. They operate in industries with high barriers to entry and exponential returns to scale.

Now consider this. What railroads were to the nineteenth century, semiconductors are to the twenty first. They are the infrastructure beneath everything. Communications. Health care. Defense. Energy. Finance. Every modern product and service either uses silicon or relies on it to function. And unlike land or oil, semiconductors do not deplete over time. They accelerate. They get smaller, faster, and more powerful. That means the value they create does not fade. It multiplies.

This is where the future lives. In design. In architecture. In intellectual leverage. Investing in this world is not a speculative bet on new technology. It is a deliberate move toward where growth is being engineered every day.

Think of it this way. Traditional real estate ties your money to a single location. A building. A tenant. A mortgage. It can work, but it scales slowly. It requires upkeep, negotiation, physical presence. Compare that to owning part of a

company like ASML, which designs the machines that allow advanced chips to be built. Or owning a stake in a company like AMD or Taiwan Semiconductor, through SMH. These businesses operate at the center of global supply chains. They sell precision, not square footage. Their products power everything from mobile phones to missile systems. And their margins are not bound by geography. They are bound only by how fast they can innovate.

The same is true for QQQ. It holds companies that create exponential value with digital leverage. They build once, sell millions of times, and improve with every iteration. They are building the future, not renting out the past. And as an investor, you can own that future. Not by guessing who wins the next earnings call, but by aligning your portfolio with the entire direction of global progress.

The real estate of this generation is not made of brick. It is made of code. The land grab is happening in artificial intelligence, in semiconductors, in cloud infrastructure. The new empire builders are engineers, designers, product architects, and platform thinkers. And the tools to participate are available to anyone with the awareness to see what is changing.

The old model said buy what you can touch. The new model says own what can scale. The old model said invest in location. The new model says invest in innovation. The old model said slow and steady wins the race. The new model says velocity compounds faster than mass.

You do not need to abandon the past. But you do need to stop anchoring your future to it.

The wealth of tomorrow will not come from buying what everyone else bought thirty years ago. It will come from owning a piece of what the world is building right now.

This is not a theory. It is already happening. And the door is open.

THE RISE OF DIGITAL INFRASTRUCTURE

WHY SEMICONDUCTORS ARE THE BACKBONE OF EVERYTHING

Imagine the world without roads, power lines, or plumbing. You would not just lose convenience. You would lose function. Societies would slow to a crawl. Businesses would stop. Communication would break. Infrastructure is not something you notice until it disappears. Then everything else starts to collapse.

That is exactly what semiconductors are in the modern world. They are the digital infrastructure beneath everything. Phones. Laptops. Cars. Hospitals. Satellites. Banks. Weapons systems. Cloud servers. Smart homes. Every modern tool and system you rely on, whether in business or daily life, runs on a silent foundation of chips. You may never see them, but without them, nothing works.

This is not an exaggeration. It is reality. The global economy has become a semiconductor economy. And yet most people still treat this sector like a niche category. As if it were just another corner of the technology market. That thinking is not just outdated. It is financially dangerous.

During the past decade, semiconductors have moved from a background role to the center of economic security, technological leadership, and national strategy. The pandemic made this clear. A global shortage of chips did not just disrupt electronics. It shut down entire industries. Automakers could not ship vehicles. Hospitals delayed equipment upgrades. Construction projects stalled. That was not just a supply chain problem. It was a strategic wake-up call.

Countries began to realize that control over chip design and production is now a matter of sovereignty. Corporations began to realize that investing in their own chip development was no longer optional. And investors began to realize that the companies powering these technologies were no longer support players. They were the core infrastructure of the next century.

To invest in semiconductors is to invest in the foundation of every growth story happening today. Artificial intelligence. Renewable energy. Space exploration. Cloud computing. Advanced medicine. Precision agriculture. None of these can scale without faster, more efficient, more powerful chips. Every breakthrough in performance or productivity begins with a leap in semiconductor design.

This is where the SMH fund comes into the picture. SMH is not just a basket of tech companies. It is a concentrated portfolio of firms at the very center of this transformation. From companies like NVIDIA, which lead in graphics processing and now artificial intelligence, to Taiwan Semiconductor, which manufactures chips for nearly every major device maker in the world, SMH gives you exposure to the architects and enablers of global innovation.

You are not betting on a trend. You are owning the platform on which every trend will depend. And unlike speculative plays that rely on hype, these companies operate with real cash flows, high demand, and technical dominance. They are building the picks and shovels for the digital gold rush. Except this time, the gold is intelligence, speed, and scalable computation.

What makes semiconductors especially powerful from an investment perspective is their dual identity. On one hand, they are physical products. They are manufactured, tested, shipped, and sold. On the other hand, they behave like intellectual property. A breakthrough in chip design can deliver a generational leap in capability, create licensing advantages, and establish years of pricing power. That combination of hardware precision and software margin structure is rare. And when you own companies that live in that zone, you own value that grows on multiple fronts.

Consider also the barriers to entry. Starting a new chip company is not like starting a new app. It takes billions in capital. Decades of research. Deep global partnerships. And extreme specialization. This keeps the playing field narrow. It limits competition. It creates moats. That kind of ecosystem is exactly where investors should want to be. Not where anyone can copy you, but where only the best in the world can even enter.

Then there is the geopolitical layer. As nations compete for technological leadership, semiconductors are at the center of trade policy, defense planning, and industrial strategy. Governments are pouring billions into domestic chip manufacturing. Alliances are being formed around chip supply chains. You do not need to predict which country will dominate. When you hold SMH, you hold the companies that everyone else is depending on.

But beyond the economic and political story lies the personal one. Every individual is becoming more digitally dependent. Your phone is your wallet, your office, your connection to the world. Your car is becoming a computer. Your house is learning your habits. Your job likely depends on data and connectivity. The smarter the world becomes, the more chips it requires. And the more chips it requires, the more valuable these companies become.

The rise of digital infrastructure is not a forecast. It is a fact. And the window to participate in it is wide open. But it will not stay open forever. As more capital flows into this space, as more governments protect it, and as more industries rely on it, the cost of entry will continue to rise. Not because of scarcity, but because of compounding value.

The best time to own digital infrastructure is before everyone realizes what it really is. Not a tech sector. Not a trend. But the new foundation of human progress.

When you invest in SMH, you are not just buying companies. You are owning the rails of the digital economy. And as that economy expands, so does your leverage.

You are not building on top of the future. You are building with it.

SOFTWARE EATS THE WORLD

QQQ'S DOMINANCE IN TECH, BIOTECH, AND PLATFORM BUSINESSES

In 2011, a visionary venture capitalist wrote a short essay with a bold headline. Software is eating the world. At the time, it felt provocative. Today, it feels obvious. Everything has become software. Your communication. Your transportation. Your health care. Your banking. Even your relationships. What used to be handled by paper, people, or physical processes has been digitized, streamlined, automated, and scaled through code.

But this transformation is not just cultural. It is economic. The most valuable companies in the world are no longer manufacturers or miners. They are platform builders. Data aggregators. Cloud architects. They deliver services through networks, not storefronts. They monetize scale, not scarcity. And they operate with margins that industrial firms could only dream of.

This is what QQQ captures. It is not just a technology fund. It is a portfolio of companies that are redefining how value is created, delivered, and multiplied. The Nasdaq one hundred is filled with firms that do not depend on physical inputs. They depend on intellectual property, engineering talent, network effects, and continuous reinvention. That is why they grow faster. That is why they dominate market share. That is why they become category kings instead of competitors in crowded markets.

Let us look at some of the companies that make up QQQ. These are names you know, but you may not fully understand how powerful they are. Companies like Apple, which no longer sells devices. It sells ecosystems of interconnected products and services. It creates recurring revenue through subscriptions, payment systems, and software bundles. Companies like Microsoft, which evolved from boxed software to a cloud platform that powers everything from small startups to Fortune 500 enterprises. Companies like Amazon, which turned retail into logistics and logistics into cloud infrastructure and cloud infrastructure into a profit engine. And then there is Alphabet, parent company of Google, which monetizes attention, organizes global information, and now leads in artificial intelligence development.

These companies do not compete based on price. They compete based on scale and speed. They win because they own the platforms everyone else has to use. And when you own QQQ, you own a slice of their success. You do not have to pick which one will outperform. You simply ride the wave of an entire innovation ecosystem moving forward together.

And QQQ is not limited to traditional tech. It includes some of the most promising biotech firms in the world. These are companies decoding the human genome, engineering precision medicine, and accelerating drug discovery with artificial intelligence. The overlap between data science and biology is becoming one of the most powerful frontiers of the next decade. And QQQ gives you access to that frontier with a single investment.

This matters for one very specific reason. In the past, you had to take extraordinary risks to get exposure to breakthrough innovation. You had to be a venture capitalist. You had to find early-stage companies. You had to tolerate massive volatility and the very real possibility of losing your entire investment. Not anymore. With QQQ, you can participate in innovation through companies that already have traction, revenue, scale, and a global footprint. You get the upside of transformation without the downside of binary outcomes.

Even more important is the structure of how these companies operate. Software companies are not bound by geography. They are not limited by distribution. Once they build something that works, they can replicate it across millions of users with almost zero marginal cost. That is the essence of leverage. That is the reason their growth can compound so aggressively. And that is why owning a portfolio of these companies is like owning a high-speed engine instead of a slow-moving machine.

Consider also the talent concentration. The best engineers in the world do not want to work at legacy firms. They want to work at companies that solve hard problems, move fast, and shape the future. QQQ is a magnet for that kind of talent. When you invest in these companies, you are investing in human capital of the highest quality. You are aligning with people who are not just building products. They are building the infrastructure of how we live, work, learn, and connect.

And yet, many investors still overlook this. They are trained to look for dividends, for low volatility, for comfort in the familiar. But the world does not reward comfort. It rewards clarity and conviction. The returns of the last twenty years have not come from playing defense. They have come from owning innovation, consistently, patiently, and with a long-term view.

QQQ is a vehicle for that ownership. It gives you exposure to the most relevant companies in the world. Companies that are not just reacting to change but driving it. Companies that are not just surviving disruption but causing it. Companies that do not need bailouts because they create their own momentum.

This is not about chasing trends. This is about understanding where the world is heading and positioning yourself accordingly. It is about reallocating your capital from systems of the past to engines of the future. QQQ is not speculation. It is alignment. Alignment with scale, with data, with intelligence, with transformation.

Software has eaten the world. The question is whether your portfolio reflects that reality. If it does not, you are investing in a version of the economy that no longer exists.

But if it does, you are not just participating in change. You are compounding with it.

LEGACY ASSETS VERSUS LIVING ASSETS

WHY SOME INVESTMENTS AGE LIKE WINE AND OTHERS LIKE MILK

Every investor holds something. A piece of property. A portfolio of stocks. A retirement account. A small business. Maybe even a paid-off home. And for many, the fact that they hold these things feels like progress. On paper, it is. But not all assets are equal. Not all ownership builds the future. Some simply preserve the past.

That is the difference between legacy assets and living assets. It is not a matter of category. It is a matter of energy. Legacy assets sit still. Living assets evolve. Legacy assets require management. Living assets generate momentum. One demands your attention. The other grows without it.

A legacy asset often feels safe because it is familiar. The rental property you can drive by. The stock your father recommended. The savings account you have had for twenty years. These things offer comfort. But comfort is not the same as compounding. Stability is not the same as performance. Some assets age gracefully. Others decay quietly while appearing respectable.

Real estate can be powerful when it is managed well and held strategically. But it is not immune to stagnation. Taxes increase. Maintenance demands attention. Tenants come and go. Regulation shifts. Liquidity remains limited. It is a legacy strategy that still works for many, but it requires a level of involvement and local knowledge that not everyone has. More importantly, its returns are often capped by its physical limitations.

Now contrast that with a living asset. A holding that evolves, adapts, scales, and compounds over time. These are businesses that reinvest their profits. Platforms that expand their user base. Networks that strengthen as they grow. Intellectual property that multiplies in value with each use. Living assets are not static. They are dynamic. They are not dependent on your labor. They are driven by innovation.

When you invest in funds like QQQ or SMH, you are not buying assets that sit quietly in the corner of your portfolio. You are buying living assets. You are buying into ecosystems that are constantly upgrading themselves. QQQ holds companies that reinvest heavily into research and development. Companies that attract the world's top talent. Companies that pivot, improve, and accelerate year after year. SMH holds companies that push the edge of technological possibility, making smaller, faster, more powerful chips that become indispensable to every sector of the global economy.

These companies do not rest. They reinvent. And when they do, your ownership compounds. Not just in price appreciation, but in future potential. You are not just holding an asset. You are holding the momentum of an entire industry that is building the future.

Living assets also have a different relationship with time. The longer you hold them, the more powerful they become. That is the essence of compounding. But with legacy assets, time can sometimes work against you. What was once a strong return becomes average as appreciation slows, taxes rise, or technology makes the asset less relevant. You may still hold it. It may still have value. But it no longer grows in a meaningful way.

This is why modern wealth builders are shifting their thinking. They are not just looking at cash flow. They are asking what is growing underneath the surface. What assets are still learning. Still scaling. Still leading. They are reallocating from familiarity to force. From static holdings to dynamic engines.

That does not mean you should abandon everything traditional. It means you must be honest about what each asset actually does for your future. Is it giving you leverage or just inertia. Is it opening up options or tying up capital. Is it compounding or is it coasting.

The economy has changed. The world moves faster. Value accrues differently. Assets that once delivered predictable returns now underperform. Meanwhile, new types of assets have emerged. Ones that reflect the pace and power of the digital age. Investing is no longer about preservation alone. It is about participation in progress.

QQQ and SMH are not just growth vehicles. They are reflections of modern value creation. They are portfolios of living assets that participate in the upside of innovation, network effects, and global scale. They require no maintenance, no property management, no legal paperwork. But they deliver something far more powerful. Exposure to companies and sectors that are still in motion.

If you want your wealth to grow, your assets must grow too. Not just in price, but in energy. In relevance. In contribution to the world around them. Look at what you own and ask yourself, is this asset alive. Is it still earning its place. Is it building my future or just preserving my past.

Because in a world that moves this fast, holding onto the past is not just inefficient. It is expensive.

THE INNOVATION FLYWHEEL

HOW TECH ACCELERATES ITS OWN VALUE AND DRIVES MARKET MOMENTUM

In the old economy, growth required more input. More factories. More labor. More raw materials. If you wanted to produce more, you needed to build more. Hire more. Spend more. Growth was linear. It was expensive. And it came with hard physical limits.

The new economy does not follow those rules. Technology grows by layering on itself. It does not require more physical space. It requires better code. Smarter models. Tighter integration. Each breakthrough becomes the foundation for the next. Each improvement reduces the cost of the next improvement. Each cycle speeds up the next cycle.

That is the innovation flywheel. And once it starts spinning, it does not slow down. It accelerates.

Think about what happens when a company like NVIDIA makes a leap in chip design. That chip enables more powerful artificial intelligence models. Those models improve software products. Those products create new user experiences and business capabilities. Those capabilities generate revenue, which flows back into research and development, allowing for even faster innovation. The loop feeds itself.

This is not just impressive. It is financially explosive.

The companies inside funds like QQQ and SMH are not simply growing. They are compounding at the level of product, performance, and platform. Their improvements unlock new markets. Their reach attracts more talent. Their scale creates cost advantages that competitors cannot match. These advantages are not temporary. They are structural. They are built into the design of the business.

This is why innovation-driven firms tend to dominate their categories. Once they get enough traction, they move beyond competition. They stop winning market share and start defining the market. That is when real wealth is created. Not from marginal improvement, but from category leadership.

Now imagine owning an entire portfolio of companies like this. Companies that do not just react to the future. They invent it. That is what QQQ and SMH offer. Exposure to an ecosystem where each company benefits from the progress of the others. Where the gains of one reinforce the momentum of many.

In traditional investing, your assets are separate. A retail stock is not connected to your industrial stock. A utility company does not boost the performance of your energy fund. But in innovation, the connections matter. A breakthrough in cloud infrastructure benefits the companies building on top of that infrastructure. A new chip architecture benefits the entire software stack that relies on faster processing. These synergies accelerate growth across the portfolio. They create force multipliers that are almost impossible to replicate in legacy sectors.

And it is not just about technology. It is about the structure of innovation itself. When a traditional business wants to grow, it faces a ceiling. It has to expand locations. Hire more people. Take on more risk. But when a software business wants to grow, it replicates itself with zero marginal cost. It pushes updates, not paperwork. It improves products through data, not guesses. The entire model compounds.

Now take that concept one step further. What happens when artificial intelligence begins to write code. When machines begin to optimize their own processes. When data trains the system in real time. You are no longer looking at a business cycle. You are looking at an intelligence cycle. A feedback loop that does not just improve the company. It evolves the entire ecosystem.

This is where the innovation flywheel becomes unstoppable. Because it is not just the companies that evolve. The market begins to price in their momentum. Investors anticipate future earnings. Talent gravitates toward opportunity. Customers become evangelists. Entire industries begin to shift toward the platforms that are setting the pace.

And the flywheel spins faster.

This is why the returns from innovation-based portfolios have outpaced nearly every other sector over the last two decades. It is not just a matter of growth. It is a matter of compounding dynamics. The winners are not just participating in progress. They are causing it. And when you invest in these firms through vehicles like QQQ and SMH, you are not watching from the sidelines. You are riding the engine.

Many investors still think in static terms. They see value as a number. A price on a screen. A quarterly report. But value in the modern economy is dynamic. It is built on motion. On iteration. On feedback loops that create second-order and third-order gains. Those gains do not show up immediately. But when they do, they arrive in waves.

That is the nature of the innovation flywheel. It builds quietly. Then moves suddenly. And when it moves, it is almost impossible to stop.

You do not need to predict which company will deliver the next breakthrough. You need to own the system that rewards every breakthrough. That is the genius of QQQ and SMH. They are not bets. They are exposure. Exposure to velocity. Exposure to momentum. Exposure to a world that accelerates itself.

Innovation does not need your permission. It does not wait for you to feel ready. But it does reward those who position themselves early. Those who understand that progress is not just coming. It is compounding.

And the flywheel is already spinning.

WHY PARKING MONEY IN THE PAST IS RISKIER THAN THE FUTURE

A WAKE-UP CALL FOR TRADITIONAL INVESTORS

There is a quiet comfort in the familiar. You know the names. You know the stories. You know how those assets performed in the past. So you stick with what feels solid. You park your money in places that have a long track record. You lean on history to guide your future. But here is the uncomfortable truth. In a world that moves this fast, history is no longer the best teacher. It is often the biggest distraction.

What worked in the past was built for a different economy. That economy rewarded capital tied to physical things. Factories. Buildings. Raw materials. Local monopolies. Linear growth. You could accumulate wealth by owning things that stood still. You could count on predictable patterns and safe yields. The system was slower. The players were fewer. The competition was local. But that world has changed. And the strategies that succeeded in it are no longer enough.

Parking your money in yesterday's assets might feel safe. But in a dynamic market, stagnation is risk. The longer you hold onto outdated investments out of comfort or nostalgia, the more opportunity you leave on the table. And that opportunity cost compounds. Not just in returns. In time. In momentum. In freedom.

Look at the companies and sectors that once dominated the economy. Many have been replaced. Not by similar versions of themselves but by entirely new models. Print newspapers were replaced by digital platforms. Taxi companies were replaced by ride-sharing apps. Retail giants were replaced by e-commerce ecosystems. Cable television was replaced by streaming services. The lesson is not that change is coming. The lesson is that change already happened. And it will happen again.

Traditional investing advice often says diversify across sectors. Hold a little of everything. Include energy. Include industrials. Include financials. But diversification without conviction becomes dilution. And if the world is clearly moving in one direction, spreading your bets evenly across old and new is not smart. It is passive. It is defensive. It assumes the future will reward every sector equally. But that is not what history shows. Innovation does not play fair. It rewards a few exponentially and leaves the rest behind.

Investing in the past is easy. The data is available. The story is clear. You know what happened. But investing in the future is where real wealth is built. That takes vision. It takes a willingness to say the world will look different tomorrow and I want to be part of it. Not as a spectator. As an owner.

This is where funds like QQQ and SMH play a critical role. They are not just high-growth vehicles. They are directional bets on where the economy is going. QQQ is full of companies that are building the digital platforms, cloud infrastructure, and artificial intelligence capabilities that the world increasingly depends on. SMH is packed with the companies designing and manufacturing the chips that power everything from electric vehicles to national defense. These are not the sidelines. These are the foundation.

And while some investors still hesitate, still cling to dividend stocks or legacy holdings, the market keeps evolving. The pace of technological progress is increasing. The speed of adoption is accelerating. The next decade will not be shaped by companies that move slowly. It will be shaped by companies that move early, iterate fast, and scale globally. You can either be part of that movement or hope your traditional portfolio can keep up.

There is another risk in parking money in the past. It trains you to expect less. You begin to believe that low returns are the price of safety. You accept mediocrity as discipline. But discipline is not about accepting low performance. It is about aligning your capital with your conviction. And if you believe the future belongs to innovation, then you must invest like it.

This is not about reckless optimism. It is about strategic alignment. It is about understanding that the world is being rebuilt around digital systems, smart machines, and scalable networks. That the companies creating this world are not just new players. They are rewriting the rules. And they are already winning.

The safest place for your money is not the place that feels comfortable. It is the place that continues to grow. The place that is relevant. Resilient. Reinventing itself. That is what modern investing demands. Not nostalgia. Not hesitation. But clarity.

Holding on to legacy assets might feel responsible. But if those assets are no longer generating real growth, they are silently pulling you backward. Every dollar you keep tied to an outdated model is a dollar that is not compounding in a system built for the future.

Wealth is not a reward for caution. It is a return on alignment. The more you align your capital with progress, the more you accelerate your financial freedom. You do not need to abandon everything traditional. But you do need to make sure the core of your portfolio is alive. Focused. Positioned.

Because in today's world, the riskiest move is not stepping forward. It is standing still.

03
MEET SMH AND QQQ

NOT JUST TICKERS, THESE ARE THE
ENGINES OF TOMORROW'S WEALTH

MAIN POINTS

» **SMH: The Silent Giant**
Understanding the semiconductor ETF and why it matters

» **QQQ: The Innovation Index**
The story behind the Nasdaq-100 and its explosive potential

» **What's Inside the Ticker?**
Breakdown of key holdings and why they're future-proof

» **Built-in Diversification**
Why these ETFs protect you without diluting growth

» **Performance You Can't Ignore**
Historical returns and the power of long-term compounding

» **Why Institutions Bet on These**
How hedge funds, endowments, and billionaires allocate

SMH THE SILENT GIANT

UNDERSTANDING THE SEMICONDUCTOR ETF AND WHY IT MATTERS

Some investments shout. They make headlines. They dominate financial news cycles. Traders chase them. Commentators dissect them. Everyone talks about them, whether they understand them or not. Other investments are quiet. They sit in the background. They do not make noise. But they build quietly. They deliver. And over time, they often outperform everything else.

SMH is one of those quiet giants.

On the surface, SMH looks simple. It is an exchange traded fund that tracks a group of leading semiconductor companies. But beneath the surface, it is one of the most strategically important investment vehicles of our generation. Not because it is trendy. Not because it is speculative. But because it gives you direct ownership in the infrastructure powering the future.

Most people do not wake up thinking about semiconductors. You do not see them. You do not touch them. You do not notice them. But they are everywhere. Every device. Every vehicle. Every network. Every system. From your phone to your thermostat to the satellite that guides your GPS. All of it runs on silicon. And the companies that design, manufacture, and supply these chips are not just participants in the global economy. They are the foundation.

This is what SMH gives you access to. The core of global progress.

It includes companies like Taiwan Semiconductor, the largest and most advanced contract chip manufacturer in the world. Without them, most of the major tech firms could not ship their products. It includes NVIDIA, the leader in graphics processing and now the dominant force in artificial intelligence hardware. It includes ASML, the only company on earth that produces the extreme ultraviolet lithography machines needed to make the most advanced chips. These are not just good companies. They are irreplaceable.

When you invest in SMH, you are not betting on a single stock. You are not picking winners. You are owning the value chain that makes digital life possible. You are positioned across design, fabrication, equipment, and testing. This built-in integration gives you exposure to every stage of innovation. And as the demand for faster, smaller, more efficient chips continues to grow, the companies inside SMH grow with it.

This is not theory. It is already happening.

Artificial intelligence is accelerating. Electric vehicles are scaling. Cloud computing is expanding. Defense systems are becoming more autonomous. Medical devices are becoming smarter. All of this depends on semiconductors. And that demand is not cyclical. It is structural. We are not just using more chips. We are becoming dependent on them in every part of our lives.

But here is what makes SMH especially powerful as an investment. The companies inside it do not just grow because the world is evolving. They grow because they are building the tools that drive that evolution. They are not following trends. They are enabling them. They are the upstream force that every other innovation relies on.

The financial profile of these companies reflects that reality. High gross margins. Strong cash flow. Technical moats. Global reach. Strategic importance. They are not just high tech. They are high quality. And the ETF structure of SMH gives you exposure to all of it with a single decision. No stock picking. No trading. Just smart ownership of a critical sector.

And while the price may fluctuate in the short term, the long-term trajectory is unmistakable. These companies are positioned at the intersection of economic growth, geopolitical strategy, and technological necessity. Governments are investing billions into chip production. Corporations are racing to secure supply. Consumers are demanding smarter, faster devices. The direction is clear. And the value is compounding.

Owning SMH is like owning a toll booth on the highway of digital progress. As more data moves. As more devices connect. As more intelligence is deployed. The companies in SMH collect the economic rent. They are not chasing trends. They are powering them.

And yet, many portfolios still ignore this. Investors flock to brand names, to media favorites, to companies with visible products. But the real opportunity lies in owning the infrastructure. The quiet enablers. The firms that make everything else possible but rarely make the headlines.

That is SMH.

It is not glamorous. But it is essential. It is not loud. But it is powerful. It is not a gamble. It is a gateway.

A gateway to own the systems, the capabilities, and the momentum of a world that is accelerating every single day.

QQQ THE INNOVATION INDEX

THE STORY BEHIND NASDAQ 100 AND ITS EXPLOSIVE POTENTIAL

There are investment products. And then there are investment ecosystems. QQQ is not just another fund. It is the flagship of innovation. It is a living portfolio that reflects how the economy has transformed and where value continues to emerge. It is structured to capture what the world is building, not just what it has built. And it does that by tracking one of the most dynamic indexes in existence, the Nasdaq one hundred.

To understand QQQ, you have to understand what it includes and, just as importantly, what it excludes.

The Nasdaq one hundred is made up of one hundred of the largest nonfinancial companies listed on the Nasdaq exchange. That means no traditional banks. No legacy insurance firms. No old-world financial players. This one decision gives the index a completely different flavor from others. It filters out the industries tied to outdated models and focuses entirely on companies that drive growth, disrupt legacy systems, and scale through technology and innovation.

QQQ gives you access to the best of these companies in a single fund. Companies that lead in cloud computing, cybersecurity, e-commerce, artificial intelligence, digital media, biotechnology, and advanced hardware. You are not just investing in the present. You are investing in velocity. In momentum. In adaptability.

The DNA of QQQ is different from traditional indexes. Most indexes are backward-looking. They reflect an economy that existed twenty years ago. They are slow to change. They are anchored in companies that move cautiously and think incrementally. QQQ is forward-facing. It rotates into leaders quickly. It rewards innovation. It replaces stagnation with growth. It does not simply mirror the market. It highlights where the market is going next.

Look at the names that dominate the fund. Microsoft. Apple. Amazon. Alphabet. NVIDIA. Meta. These are not just large companies. They are platforms. They are economies within the economy. They shape consumer behavior, influence policy, drive infrastructure, and direct the flow of capital and talent around the globe.

When Microsoft launches a new artificial intelligence integration, it impacts millions of users instantly. When Amazon builds new logistics systems, it shifts how global supply chains operate. When Apple rolls out a software update, it reshapes privacy, payments, and app ecosystems. These are not marginal moves. They are structural shifts. And QQQ gives you access to them at scale.

But the power of QQQ goes beyond the household names. The fund includes a wide range of high-growth companies in biotech, semiconductors, data analytics, and automation. Many of these firms are not yet widely known, but they are leading in their categories. They are developing treatments for rare diseases. They are building the chips that will power the next wave of artificial intelligence. They are building the software that automates knowledge work. Owning QQQ means you own those possibilities before they become headlines.

Another unique aspect of QQQ is its exposure to optionality. These companies do not just have strong products. They have strong balance sheets, loyal customer bases, and the capacity to enter new markets rapidly. When NVIDIA decides to shift deeper into data centers, it brings with it a competitive advantage that few can match. When Meta invests in virtual and augmented reality, it brings billions of users and the resources to experiment until it gets it right. This kind of optionality creates new revenue streams, deepens moats, and accelerates compounding growth.

From an investment perspective, QQQ offers a powerful blend of stability and upside. The large cap companies provide resilience. The mid-tier growth companies offer acceleration. The fund as a whole behaves like a diversified innovation engine. It is constantly evolving. It is self-refreshing. It is adaptive by design. That means your investment remains aligned with the most relevant trends in the economy, even as those trends evolve.

And the performance speaks for itself. Over the past two decades, QQQ has consistently outperformed most major benchmarks. Not because of luck. Because of structure. It is built to reflect where the real growth is happening. And it avoids the drag of industries that no longer deliver. That structural advantage compounds over time.

QQQ is also widely used by institutional investors. Pension funds, hedge funds, endowments, and sovereign wealth funds allocate to QQQ because they know what it represents. It is not just a technology bet. It is a directional investment in the modern economy. It is a signal that you understand what matters now and what will matter next.

For the individual investor, QQQ offers something even more important than performance. It offers clarity. Clarity about what kind of future you want to own. Clarity about which parts of the economy are growing and which are shrinking. Clarity about how to align your capital with your beliefs.

You do not need to build a portfolio from scratch. You do not need to analyze hundreds of earnings reports. You need to own what is building the future. QQQ makes that possible. Simply. Effectively. Strategically.

This is not just an index. It is a philosophy. A philosophy of progress. A philosophy of alignment. A philosophy of taking ownership in the companies and capabilities that will define the next ten, twenty, even thirty years.

QQQ is not for those who are afraid of change. It is for those who want to benefit from it. It is for those who understand that the world will not slow down. And neither should your investment strategy.

WHAT'S INSIDE THE TICKER

BREAKDOWN OF KEY HOLDINGS AND WHY THEY ARE FUTURE PROOF

Most people look at a fund and see a symbol. Four letters. A price. A performance chart. But behind every ticker is a strategy. A structure. A philosophy about where the world is heading. If you want to understand why SMH and QQQ are two of the most effective vehicles for building wealth in the modern economy, you need to look beyond the surface. You need to see what is inside.

Let us start with SMH.

SMH is the VanEck Semiconductor ETF. It is composed of companies that are essential to the design, production, and development of semiconductors. This is not a broad tech fund. It is a precise, concentrated allocation to the firms that are quite literally powering the digital age.

One of the largest holdings is Taiwan Semiconductor Manufacturing Company. This firm produces the most advanced chips in the world. Apple, AMD, and even NVIDIA rely on them to manufacture their high-performance products. Their technological lead is unmatched. Their scale is global. And they are irreplaceable in the current supply chain.

Another key player is NVIDIA. Originally known for graphics cards in gaming, NVIDIA now leads the world in chips designed for artificial intelligence, data centers, and advanced computing. Their architecture is the engine behind machine learning models, autonomous vehicles, and scientific simulations. Owning NVIDIA is not about gaming. It is about exponential computation.

Then there is ASML, a Dutch company that builds the extreme ultraviolet lithography machines used to manufacture the most advanced semiconductors. These machines are so complex and so essential that ASML holds a monopoly on their production. Without ASML, the global chip industry would stall. That is not an exaggeration. That is a strategic reality.

Other top holdings include Texas Instruments, Broadcom, Intel, and Qualcomm. These companies span a wide range of functions. Analog chips. Wireless communication. Power management. Embedded systems. Together they form an ecosystem that supports smartphones, cloud infrastructure, defense systems, transportation, and much more.

SMH is not just a diversified set of names. It is an integrated bet on the most critical layer of the global economy. A layer that is growing in demand, increasing in complexity, and rising in strategic importance. These companies do not just benefit from growth. They enable it.

Now let us look at QQQ.

QQQ is the Invesco Nasdaq one hundred ETF. It tracks the top one hundred nonfinancial companies listed on the Nasdaq exchange. That sounds simple. But what it really means is that you are gaining exposure to the most innovative, agile, and scalable companies in the world.

At the top of the list is Apple. A company that generates more revenue from services and ecosystems than from devices. Its ability to design, integrate, and monetize across hardware, software, and digital platforms is unparalleled.

Next is Microsoft. Once known for its Windows operating system, it now dominates cloud computing through Azure, productivity software through Office, and enterprise security through its cloud ecosystem. Microsoft is no longer just a software company. It is a digital infrastructure company.

Then comes Amazon. More than a retailer, Amazon is the backbone of e-commerce logistics and the global leader in cloud computing through Amazon Web Services. AWS alone generates billions in profit and supports everything from startups to global banks.

Alphabet, the parent company of Google, is also a top holding. It monetizes attention through advertising, organizes global knowledge, and continues to lead in artificial intelligence research. With platforms like YouTube, Google Cloud, and Android, Alphabet has massive reach and leverage.

NVIDIA is also in QQQ, reinforcing how core technologies like semiconductors appear across multiple innovation layers. This cross-pollination creates a reinforcing effect. The growth of one company enables the growth of others.

The fund also includes Meta Platforms, the company behind Facebook, Instagram, and WhatsApp. While its recent investments in virtual and augmented reality have drawn attention, its scale in communication and digital advertising remains enormous.

Outside of big tech, QQQ includes leaders in biotech such as Amgen and Gilead Sciences. It includes data companies like Adobe and Salesforce. It includes hardware innovators like Intel and automation firms like Intuitive Surgical. These are not speculative plays. They are category leaders with proven products, global footprints, and strong balance sheets.

What makes both SMH and QQQ so powerful is not just what they hold. It is how those holdings evolve. These ETFs are dynamic. They refresh. Underperformers are removed. Leaders rise. This ensures that your capital stays aligned with innovation, not with inertia.

You are not just owning stocks. You are owning capabilities. Cloud infrastructure. Artificial intelligence. Digital platforms. Semiconductor manufacturing. Cybersecurity. Precision medicine. Each of these sectors is not only growing but reshaping entire industries.

Traditional portfolios often include companies because they once mattered. SMH and QQQ include companies because they still matter and will continue to matter even more. They are designed not for nostalgia but for relevance. Not for defense but for direction.

This is what sits inside the ticker. Not symbols. Not speculation. Strategic assets that reflect the future of productivity, intelligence, connectivity, and value creation.

When you invest in SMH or QQQ, you are not placing a bet. You are planting your capital inside ecosystems that are expanding, evolving, and accelerating. You are choosing alignment over assumption. You are choosing motion over memory. You are choosing to build with the world instead of watching from the sidelines.

And the best part is that the work is already being done for you. The research. The rebalancing. The reinvestment. You simply need to step in and stay committed.

Because what sits inside these tickers is not just innovation. It is your access to the future.

BUILT-IN DIVERSIFICATION

WHY THESE ETFS PROTECT YOU WITHOUT DILUTING GROWTH

For decades, investors have been told to diversify. Spread the risk. Do not put all your eggs in one basket. Own a little bit of everything. This advice sounds safe. It sounds balanced. But in a world where value is no longer evenly distributed, it can also be misleading.

Diversification is not about holding more. It is about holding what matters. True diversification is not just about the number of holdings. It is about the quality of the exposure. The relevance of the assets. The ability of those assets to grow and protect you in a world that does not move in straight lines.

Too many investors end up with portfolios that are over-diversified and underperforming. They own dozens of positions across multiple sectors, but most of those positions are anchored in legacy industries with limited upside. The result is a diluted portfolio. Low volatility, yes. But also low growth. Low energy. Low conviction.

This is where SMH and QQQ change the game.

These funds offer a different kind of diversification. A smarter kind. A built-in system that spreads risk without sacrificing direction. They are not trying to mirror the entire economy. They are focused on the most dynamic, innovative, and strategically critical segments of the economy. And they do so by selecting leaders within those segments, not just filling space for the sake of balance.

Start with SMH.

SMH holds companies across the semiconductor value chain. This includes chip designers, manufacturers, equipment providers, and integrated device makers. You are not exposed to just one part of the process. You are exposed to the entire ecosystem. If a chip shortage slows manufacturing, companies focused on equipment and design may benefit. If demand spikes for artificial intelligence processing, companies that build the required graphics chips will see growth. This internal diversity creates resilience. It allows for strength in one area to balance short-term weakness in another.

But what makes SMH truly unique is that the companies inside it are not competitors in the traditional sense. They are collaborators in a global supply chain. Each one plays a distinct role. Each one captures value in a different way. This is diversification by design. Not by volume. Not by randomness. By architecture.

Now look at QQQ.

With one fund, you gain exposure to one hundred of the most powerful nonfinancial companies in the Nasdaq. These companies operate across cloud computing, e-commerce, biotechnology, cybersecurity, social media, artificial intelligence, software, semiconductors, and digital communications. You are diversified across industries, but only within the most adaptive corner of the economy.

And because QQQ is market-cap weighted, your exposure is intelligently concentrated. The larger, more established companies carry more weight. These are the firms with proven models, global scale, and financial strength. But the fund also includes smaller players with faster growth trajectories. That balance gives you both stability and acceleration. Both consistency and asymmetry.

This is a key distinction. Traditional diversification treats every company as equal. QQQ recognizes that all companies are not equal. Some are structurally advantaged. Some are strategically positioned. Some have business models that scale faster, generate more margin, and reinvest more aggressively. Owning more companies is not the goal. Owning better companies is.

That is what makes these ETFs different from an index like the S and P 500. The S and P 500 includes energy companies, utilities, banks, and manufacturers. These sectors have their place, but they do not drive the future. They do not scale like software. They do not innovate like biotech. They do not accelerate like artificial intelligence. If you want to grow with the economy, you need to own the parts of the economy that are growing.

Built-in diversification does not mean avoiding risk. It means managing risk while preserving your upside. SMH and QQQ do this exceptionally well. They give you exposure to multiple companies, multiple industries, multiple revenue streams, and multiple business models. But they are all aligned around a central idea. The world is changing fast, and value now flows to those who can move with it.

That is what real diversification looks like in the modern economy. Not scattering your bets. But concentrating on the right ecosystems. Ecosystems that are adaptive. Resilient. And positioned to benefit from the biggest shifts in how we live, work, and communicate.

With SMH, you own the digital infrastructure. With QQQ, you own the platforms built on top of that infrastructure. Together, they give you depth and breadth. They give you foundational exposure and exponential opportunity. They give you a portfolio that is not only diversified but strategically aligned with where the future is going.

And you can do it all with two funds. Two decisions. No guesswork. No noise.

Diversification does not need to be complicated. It needs to be intelligent.

Own what is relevant. Own what is moving. Own what is building.

That is built-in diversification that actually works.

PERFORMANCE YOU CANNOT IGNORE

HISTORICAL RETURNS AND THE POWER OF LONG-TERM COMPOUNDING

Every investment decision carries a question behind it. Will this work. Can I trust it. Will it actually build wealth over time. These are not abstract concerns. They are fundamental to how people allocate their savings, their future, and their belief in what is possible.

There is a popular saying in investing. Past performance is not indicative of future results. That warning is important when used as a caution against chasing trends or falling for hype. But when performance is backed by structural forces, long-term trends, and repeatable business models, history becomes more than a mirror. It becomes a compass.

The historical performance of SMH and QQQ is not just strong. It is remarkable. And more important than the numbers themselves is the **why** behind those numbers.

Start with QQQ.

QQQ has consistently outperformed traditional benchmarks like the S and P 500 over the past ten, fifteen, and twenty years. It has done this through multiple market cycles. It has weathered recessions, interest rate hikes, inflation shocks, and geopolitical events. And through all of it, the companies inside QQQ have continued to grow, innovate, and compound.

The fund is filled with firms that turn investment into innovation. They reinvest heavily into research and development. They build platforms, not just products. They create ecosystems, not just transactions. As a result, their growth is not just a reflection of market timing. It is a reflection of value creation at scale.

Apple redefined what a phone could be and built an entire services economy on top of it. Microsoft transformed from a software provider into a cloud leader. Amazon moved from online retail into global logistics and artificial intelligence. Alphabet scaled advertising into information infrastructure. NVIDIA moved from gaming chips to powering the artificial intelligence revolution.

These companies do not just participate in the economy. They shape it. And QQQ captures that shaping force with precision. That is why the returns have not only been strong but consistent. QQQ is not a rocket. It is a compounding engine.

Now turn to SMH.

Semiconductors have become the core driver of every major technological wave. From personal computing to mobile devices. From cloud infrastructure to artificial intelligence. From automotive innovation to defense systems. Chips power it all. And the companies that make up SMH are not just riding these trends. They are enabling them.

That is why SMH has also delivered extraordinary returns over time. It reflects a concentrated bet on the most important layer of digital infrastructure. And that bet has been rewarded. SMH has outperformed broader market indexes during the most dynamic periods of technological advancement. And it has done so with companies that combine technical dominance with financial strength.

These are firms with high gross margins, deep intellectual property, strong pricing power, and global demand. When a company like ASML becomes the sole provider of a tool required to produce next-generation chips, that company is not just valuable. It is essential. When Taiwan Semiconductor becomes the manufacturing arm of the global tech industry, its returns are not just financial. They are strategic.

These are not speculative companies. These are foundational assets. And SMH gives you exposure to all of them in one fund.

Now consider the long-term impact of compounding. Even small differences in annual return create massive differences over time. A portfolio that grows at ten percent annually will double roughly every seven years. At fifteen percent, it doubles in under five. Over twenty or thirty years, that gap becomes life changing.

This is why performance matters. Not as a scorecard. But as a signal.

A signal that you are allocating capital into systems that build. Systems that grow. Systems that reinvest and return value over and over again.

Many investors settle for average because they are told not to expect more. But SMH and QQQ show that more is possible when you stop chasing headlines and start aligning with real momentum.

The beauty of these funds is that you do not need to be a stock picker. You do not need to guess which company will dominate next. You own the entire curve of innovation. The entire layer of infrastructure. The entire engine of reinvention.

You are not just buying a fund. You are buying the historical performance of world-class businesses. Businesses that have already proven they can scale. Businesses that continue to deliver in changing conditions. Businesses that are positioned to keep compounding well into the future.

And yes, markets will fluctuate. There will be corrections. There will be volatility. That is part of the journey. But when you zoom out, the trajectory tells the story. It is not a straight line. But it is an upward one.

Ignore the short-term noise. Focus on the long-term structure. Because that structure has already delivered. And it is still just getting started.

When it comes to SMH and QQQ, the performance is not just strong. It is a lesson. A lesson in what happens when you own the right companies for long enough. A lesson in what is possible when you stop reacting and start positioning.

And most of all, a lesson in what it looks like to put your money where the future is already being built.

HOW HEDGE FUNDS, ENDOWMENTS, AND BILLIONAIRES ALLOCATE

When it comes to investing, most people follow advice. Institutions follow strategy.

There is a fundamental difference between how the average investor approaches the market and how professional capital allocators think. Individuals are often emotional. They react to headlines. They get distracted by noise. They search for quick wins or safe havens. Institutions operate on an entirely different level. They do not chase. They position. They think in decades. They manage risk through design, not through fear. And they allocate based on conviction, not convenience.

This is why it is so important to watch where institutional capital flows. Not because it is always perfect. But because it reveals what the most informed investors believe about where the future is going. And again and again, that capital points toward SMH and QQQ.

Start with endowments.

University endowments are some of the most well-capitalized and strategically managed funds in the world. Schools like Harvard, Stanford, Yale, and MIT manage tens of billions of dollars on behalf of future generations. Their mission is not to beat the market in the short term. Their mission is to preserve and grow wealth over the long term. And their allocation decisions reflect that purpose.

You will find that these endowments consistently allocate toward technology and innovation. They hold public equities that include companies inside QQQ. Many also hold private positions that mirror the sectors represented in SMH. These are not speculative plays. They are long-term exposures to the most productive assets in the economy. Institutions allocate here because they know the future is being built in code, in chips, in platforms, in systems that scale.

Next come the hedge funds.

The most elite hedge funds manage not only massive amounts of capital, but also enormous reputational risk. They are judged by performance, discipline, and timing. And still, many of them hold concentrated positions in firms like NVIDIA, Apple, Microsoft, and Amazon. These firms are among the top holdings in QQQ. Others focus specifically on semiconductors, recognizing the strategic leverage these companies hold. They do not just follow the crowd. They move early, go deep, and hold strong.

Some hedge funds even build strategies around volatility within SMH and QQQ. They use options, leverage, and derivatives to enhance exposure or hedge positions, but the core bet remains the same. The innovation economy continues to produce outlier results. And they want to own those outcomes at scale.

Pension funds and sovereign wealth funds offer a different lens.

These funds are responsible for national stability. They fund retirements, infrastructure, and large-scale public programs. They cannot afford to chase hype. They must allocate with discipline and foresight. Yet they, too, have increasingly moved capital into innovation-heavy funds. Many use QQQ and similar vehicles as core positions. Not fringe bets. Core holdings.

Why would funds managing hundreds of billions of dollars bet on QQQ and SMH? Because they understand something most individual investors overlook.

These funds offer asymmetric return potential. That means the upside is significant while the long-term downside risk is mitigated through diversification, liquidity, and the quality of the underlying companies. They are not fragile bets. They are engineered for strength, even under pressure.

And they offer something else. They align with the global direction of value creation.

Institutions see where the smartest people are working. Where the capital is flowing. Where the infrastructure is being built. Where the next generation of economic value will be concentrated. And they want to own it. Not watch it. Not rent it. Own it.

SMH represents the companies that are powering every layer of that infrastructure. From the servers to the sensors to the satellites. QQQ represents the platforms that are changing how we communicate, learn, transact, heal, and live. These are not optional investments anymore. They are essential allocations for any entity that wants to remain relevant, resilient, and exposed to growth.

What can an individual investor learn from this?

You do not need a billion-dollar fund to think like one. You do not need a finance team to understand what the best capital allocators already know. You simply need to follow the principle.

Own what is building the future. Own what delivers asymmetric returns. Own what institutions buy not because they are chasing performance, but because they are positioning for longevity.

When you build your portfolio with SMH and QQQ, you are not just following trends. You are aligning with the investment philosophy of those who manage the world's most serious capital.

You are stepping into a strategy that has already earned the confidence of the world's most sophisticated investors.

That confidence is earned for a reason.

Because SMH and QQQ are not just vehicles. They are blueprints.

They are what the future of smart investing looks like when you remove the noise, do the work, and position yourself with clarity.

And now that you know what the best investors already know, the only question left is whether you will follow that clarity into action.

04
THE PSYCHOLOGY OF WEALTH BUILDING

WIN THE MENTAL GAME, OR
THE MARKET WILL WIN AGAINST YOU

MAIN POINTS

» **FOMO, Fear, and Financial Paralysis**
How emotions sabotage smart investing

» **Time in the Market Beats Timing the Market**
The myth of perfect entry points

» **Discipline Over Drama**
Why consistent investing outperforms high-conviction trades

» **The Dopamine Problem**
How short-term thinking kills long-term wealth

» **You Are Not Your Portfolio's Daily Balance**
Detaching identity from volatility

» **How the Wealthy Stay Calm in Chaos**
Mental models for staying the course

FOMO, FEAR, AND FINANCIAL PARALYSIS

HOW EMOTIONS SABOTAGE SMART INVESTING

The hardest part of building wealth is not technical. It is not about knowing the perfect entry point or finding the next breakthrough company. It is not about reading balance sheets or tracking economic cycles. The hardest part is psychological.

Because money is never just about math. It is about emotion. It is about identity. It is about what we fear, what we crave, and what we think will protect us or elevate us. For many investors, the real challenge is not market volatility. It is emotional volatility. The market moves up and down. That is expected. What creates damage is how we respond.

At the center of that response are two forces. Fear of missing out and fear of losing everything. These forces create a cycle that feels rational in the moment but becomes destructive over time. One minute you are watching the market climb and feeling left behind. The next minute you are watching it fall and feeling like everything is at risk. So you buy high and sell low. Or you do nothing at all, paralyzed by the idea that whatever move you make might be the wrong one.

This is financial paralysis. And it is one of the most common killers of long-term wealth.

Fear of missing out makes you rush. It makes you chase the hot stock or the headline trade. You see others posting gains. You feel behind. You want to catch up. So you abandon your plan, you take on more risk than you understand, and you enter the market emotionally instead of strategically.

Then the market turns. Or the price drops. Or the gains take longer than expected. And suddenly the other fear kicks in. The fear of losing. So you pull back. You sell. You hesitate. You convince yourself that waiting is safer. But waiting without action becomes its own risk. Because the cost of not investing is invisible. It does not make noise. It just compounds in the background, silently draining your future.

This emotional cycle traps even smart people. Because it is not about intelligence. It is about biology. Your brain was not built for long-term investing. It was built to survive in a world where danger was immediate and constant. So when the market moves, your nervous system reacts. It floods you with stress signals. Fight or flight. Chase or freeze.

The irony is that the greatest opportunities in investing often feel the most uncomfortable. Market lows feel terrifying, but they are often the best entry points. Market highs feel exciting, but they often invite overconfidence. In both cases, the emotional signal is rarely aligned with the optimal move.

That is why building wealth is not just about strategy. It is about emotional discipline. It is about learning to recognize the signal beneath the noise. It is about building a mindset that can sit still while others panic. That can commit while others hesitate. That can stay the course when the world feels chaotic.

The market will always test your emotions. It will present fear in a thousand forms. Fear of missing the next rally. Fear of entering at the wrong time. Fear of holding through volatility. Fear of not doing what everyone else is doing. But behind each of these fears is a deeper question.

Do you trust your process more than you fear the outcome.

That is the turning point. Because once you shift your focus from prediction to process, everything changes. You no longer chase. You build. You no longer panic. You position. You no longer hope the market will validate your feelings. You rely on your principles to guide your actions.

This is where funds like SMH and QQQ are especially powerful. They remove a layer of emotion from the equation. You do not need to pick the perfect stock. You do not need to time the perfect moment. You are investing in long-term innovation, structural advantage, and economic relevance. That clarity allows you to commit. To stay in the game even when your emotions want to pull you out.

And when you stay in the game, you give compounding a chance to do its work. You stop reacting and start accumulating. You stop swinging and start winning.

So the next time you feel that pull, the rush to jump in because others are winning or the urge to pull out because you fear losing: Pause. Ask yourself what kind of investor you want to be. Do you want to build real wealth, or do you want to feel momentarily safe. Do you want to grow your future, or do you want to protect your ego.

Fear will always be part of investing. The question is whether it will control you or inform you. Whether it will drive your decisions or remind you to return to your plan.

The investors who win over time are not the ones who master the market. They are the ones who master themselves.

And that mastery begins the moment you stop following emotions and start following conviction.

TIME IN THE MARKET BEATS TIMING THE MARKET

THE MYTH OF PERFECT ENTRY POINTS

Every investor wants to buy low and sell high. The idea feels intuitive. Wait for the right moment. Get in at the bottom. Get out at the top. That is how you win. So people watch the news. They track charts. They wait for confirmation. They search for the signal that says now is the time.

But the truth is this. The people who spend their time trying to perfectly time the market almost always lose to the people who simply stay in the market.

Because while price matters, time matters more. While entry points can influence returns, participation determines whether you get those returns in the first place. The greatest risk to wealth is not choosing the wrong moment. It is not being invested when the moment happens.

The myth of perfect timing is one of the most expensive lies in investing. It convinces people that if they wait long enough, they can avoid all downside and capture all the upside. But markets do not work like that. The best days often follow the worst days. The biggest rallies come when fear is highest. And the cost of missing just a handful of key days can set your portfolio back years.

Study after study shows that investors who try to jump in and out of the market end up with lower returns than those who stay committed. Not because they are not smart. But because they are trying to play a game that cannot be won consistently. They think they are managing risk, but they are actually compounding indecision.

This is why the principle of time in the market is so powerful. It removes the guesswork. It focuses on what you can control. It aligns your actions with the mathematics of compounding. Because compound growth does not reward precision. It rewards consistency. It rewards patience. It rewards the investor who stays invested even when the headlines are loud and the future feels uncertain.

Consider this. Over a twenty-year period, missing just the ten best days in the market can cut your returns in half. Ten days out of more than five thousand trading sessions. And most of those best days are clustered around periods of high volatility. They are impossible to predict. They are easy to miss if you are trying to wait out the storm. But if you are consistently invested, you are there when it happens.

This is what makes funds like SMH and QQQ such powerful tools for long-term investors. They give you exposure to companies that continue to grow, adapt, and lead through multiple cycles. You do not need to guess when artificial intelligence will hit its peak adoption. You do not need to predict when semiconductors will hit a new supply surge. You simply need to stay invested in the systems that are building the future. Over time, those systems generate value. And that value compounds.

Trying to time the market can also erode your confidence. You make a move, then second-guess it. You miss a rally, then chase the next one. You sell out of fear, then hesitate to re-enter. The cycle never ends. And all the while, your capital sits on the sidelines, doing nothing.

But when you shift your focus to time in the market, your perspective changes. You stop looking for the perfect moment and start looking for strong systems. You stop asking if today is the bottom and start asking if this investment aligns with the future. You stop treating investing like a game and start treating it like a craft.

There will always be reasons to wait. The economy feels uncertain. Interest rates are rising. A new election is coming. A global conflict is unfolding. There is always a headline that says not yet. But wealth is not built in perfect conditions. It is built through conviction. Through alignment. Through action.

This does not mean you invest recklessly. It means you build a strategy that you can commit to. A system that reflects your goals, your values, and your time horizon. Then you let that system run. You refine it. You contribute to it. You trust it. And you stop trying to outguess a market that no one can predict with precision.

The most successful investors are not the best timers. They are the most consistent builders. They know that time in the market turns volatility into opportunity. They know that discipline outperforms accuracy. They know that patience compounds in ways that timing never can.

So stop waiting for the perfect signal. Stop hoping for the perfect dip. Stop worrying about what will happen tomorrow.

Start investing in what will still matter ten years from now.

Because the future will not reward timing. It will reward presence. It will reward participation.

It will reward the investor who stays.

DISCIPLINE OVER DRAMA

WHY CONSISTENT INVESTING OUTPERFORMS HIGH CONVICTION TRADES

Investing is not supposed to be exciting. That statement goes against the way most people approach markets. They want action. They want energy. They want the story of a trade that doubled overnight or a bet that turned five thousand into five hundred thousand. The drama of markets is addictive. The volatility creates adrenaline. The headlines keep us engaged.

But here is the truth that few want to hear. The best investors are not thrill seekers. They are not chasing the next big moment. They are not trying to be brilliant. They are trying to be disciplined.

Because when it comes to building wealth, consistency beats intensity. Process beats excitement. Time beats timing. The investor who makes steady contributions to strong positions will almost always outperform the investor who waits for the perfect trade and tries to go all in.

High conviction trades make for great stories. They rarely make for great outcomes. Because conviction without discipline becomes bias. It makes you double down when you should step back. It makes you ignore signals that do not fit your thesis. It makes you emotional when you need to be calm.

Discipline, on the other hand, is quiet. It does not get attention. It does not go viral. But it works. It builds. It compounds. It does not care about noise. It only cares about alignment. It asks whether this decision fits the plan. Whether this action supports the strategy. Whether this position strengthens the system.

Discipline shows up every month with another contribution. It reinvests dividends instead of spending them. It sticks to the schedule even when the market is down. It keeps the allocation consistent. It lets winners run. It does not panic when the screen turns red. It does not celebrate when the screen turns green. It simply keeps moving forward.

And over time, that forward motion becomes power.

This is the kind of investor discipline that works especially well with funds like SMH and QQQ. These are not meant to be traded like penny stocks. They are designed to be held. They are vehicles for owning long-term growth across sectors that are leading the global economy. When you invest in them consistently, regardless of market conditions, you create a system that does not rely on you being right all the time. It only relies on you showing up.

You do not need to find the bottom. You need to keep buying. You do not need to predict the peak. You need to keep holding. You do not need to outperform every year. You need to participate every year. And when you look back after ten or twenty years, you will not remember every market dip or every earnings miss. You will remember the curve. The curve that bends upward because you stayed with it.

Most people give up on their investing plan not because the plan is broken, but because their emotions are louder than their process. They feel like they are missing out. They feel like they should be doing more. So they chase. They tweak. They abandon the system. And they lose the momentum they were starting to build.

Discipline is not natural. It must be trained. It must be chosen. It must be reinforced by something stronger than the desire to react. That is why great investors often focus more on rules than on predictions. They automate their contributions. They rebalance on schedule. They define their goals. They simplify their allocations. They do not try to be smarter than the market. They try to be more consistent than the average investor.

Because consistency is the edge.

The market rewards discipline over time. It punishes drama. Drama may feel powerful. But it burns energy. It breeds mistakes. It erodes trust in the process. It pulls focus away from what matters. The market has always gone through cycles. But over the long term, it has rewarded those who stay, who hold, who build.

So the question is simple.

Do you want to impress people or do you want to build wealth. Do you want the excitement of speculation or the compounding of ownership. Do you want to be entertained or do you want to be free.

The path to freedom is not flashy. It is not dramatic. It is not chaotic.

It is steady. It is disciplined. It is quiet.

But it works.

THE DOPAMINE PROBLEM
HOW SHORT-TERM THINKING KILLS LONG-TERM WEALTH

The greatest threat to wealth is not volatility. It is not inflation. It is not interest rates or political uncertainty or even market crashes. The greatest threat to wealth is short-term thinking. And short-term thinking is not just a habit. It is a chemical addiction.

That addiction is driven by dopamine.

Dopamine is the brain's reward chemical. It fuels desire. It makes you chase. It makes you scroll. It makes you refresh your portfolio a hundred times a day. It is the reason you check your phone when you are not expecting a message. It is the reason you feel excited when a stock you own jumps and anxious when it falls. It is not rational. It is neurological.

In a world designed around screens, notifications, updates, and newsfeeds, your brain is constantly being pulled into the present moment. Not the thoughtful present. The compulsive one. The one that wants to act right now. The one that wants to feel something right now. The one that cannot sit still long enough to let compound interest do its quiet work.

This is the dopamine problem.

It makes you overreact to small moves. It makes you abandon long-term plans for short-term satisfaction. It makes you chase volatility instead of value. It makes you sell on fear and buy on hype. It turns investing into entertainment. And once that shift happens, discipline disappears.

This is not just a theory. It is a documented behavior. Behavioral finance studies have shown again and again that individual investors underperform the very funds they invest in. Not because the funds are broken. Because the investors cannot stay still. They jump in and out. They trade on emotion. They turn long-term holdings into short-term trades. The result is lower returns and higher stress.

That gap between fund performance and investor performance is not a knowledge gap. It is a behavior gap. And dopamine is often the reason.

The modern financial environment is not helping. In fact, it is making it worse. Real-time market data. Portfolio apps. Social media feeds filled with stock picks and crypto wins.

Everyone sharing their highlights. No one sharing their losses. The result is a culture of financial urgency. A belief that if you are not moving constantly, you are falling behind.

But building wealth is not a race. It is not a show. It is not a stream of wins to be shared and compared.

Building wealth is a craft. A long, slow, intentional discipline. And to succeed at it, you must learn to manage your biology.

You must learn to separate the feeling of action from the value of action. You must learn to sit with discomfort. To hold through noise. To delay gratification when the entire system is telling you to indulge.

This is where strategy becomes more than structure. It becomes protection. A clear investing plan is not just a roadmap. It is a shield against emotional sabotage. When you decide in advance how much you will invest, where you will allocate it, and when you will review it, you reduce the space where dopamine can hijack your judgment.

That is also why investing in structured vehicles like SMH and QQQ is so powerful. You are not trading headlines. You are not betting on the flavor of the month. You are owning companies that build, grow, and compound over time. These funds are not designed to entertain you. They are designed to free you.

They give you a way to invest that aligns with long-term goals, not short-term emotions. They take the pressure off the daily scoreboard. They allow you to step back, zoom out, and focus on what actually builds wealth. Not clicks. Not charts. Not commentary.

Just ownership. Just growth. Just consistency.

The investors who win in the long run are not the ones who get the biggest dopamine hit. They are the ones who learn to delay it. Who understand that the true reward is not the spike of a stock. It is the shift in your future. The moment when your money begins to buy your time. The moment when your portfolio buys your freedom.

Dopamine will not go away. It is part of being human. But it does not have to drive the bus. You can learn to observe it. Respect it. And then choose something better.

Choose peace over impulse. Choose process over reaction. Choose wealth over entertainment.

Because the goal is not to feel good for a moment. The goal is to feel free for a lifetime.

YOU ARE NOT YOUR PORTFOLIO'S DAILY BALANCE

DETACHING IDENTITY FROM VOLATILITY

Every investor checks their portfolio. At first it feels responsible. You want to know how your money is doing. You want to feel connected to your progress. But slowly and quietly something begins to shift. You stop looking for information. You start looking for identity. And once that line is crossed, the journey toward wealth becomes an emotional trap.

You are not your portfolio. But the world teaches you otherwise.

When your balance goes up, you feel successful. You feel smart. You feel ahead. When it goes down, you feel anxious. You question yourself. You lose confidence. The same plan that felt brilliant last week now feels reckless. The same asset that felt powerful now feels fragile. Not because anything fundamental changed. But because the number changed. The screen changed. The emotion changed.

This is how volatility steals energy. Not just financially. Emotionally. Mentally. Even physically. It pulls you into a feedback loop where your sense of self rises and falls with something you cannot control.

But real wealth is not built in that state. Real wealth is built when you stop using your portfolio as a mirror and start using it as a tool. A tool that serves your goals. A tool that works in the background while you live your life. A tool that moves, fluctuates, grows, and sometimes declines, but never defines who you are.

This detachment is not apathy. It is clarity. It is emotional independence. It is the ability to hold conviction through noise. To stay invested without becoming personally entangled in every daily swing.

Because portfolios do not grow in straight lines. They rise. They fall. They move sideways. They surprise. And none of that movement changes the integrity of your plan if the plan is built well. The danger comes when your identity becomes tethered to those movements.

Think about what happens when a portfolio drops ten percent. For many investors, that drop becomes a story. I am bad at this. I am losing everything. I made the wrong choice. I am behind. These are not financial statements. These are personal judgments. And those judgments lead to reactive behavior. Selling too soon. Waiting too long. Changing strategies without reason. Starting over instead of staying the course.

But the drop is not personal. The market does not know you exist. It is not attacking you. It is not testing you. It is doing what it has always done. It moves. Sometimes violently. Sometimes quietly. But always in motion. Your job is not to control that motion. Your job is to control your response.

That is what emotional separation gives you. A gap between the event and the reaction. A pause. A moment to remember what you are really doing. Building wealth over years. Owning great companies. Participating in progress. Creating freedom.

Funds like SMH and QQQ are designed for that purpose. They are not there to make you feel good every day. They are there to position your capital inside engines of long-term value. And when you hold them, your job is not to track their every tick. Your job is to remember why you own them.

You own them because technology is driving the global economy. You own them because semiconductors are the foundation of every modern system. You own them because software and platforms are scaling faster than any industrial model in history. You own them because you want to own the future, not rent it.

Once you remember that, the daily balance loses its power.

You can check it. But you do not need to react to it. You can watch it drop. But you do not need to panic. You can see it rise. But you do not need to overreach. The number becomes data. Not identity.

This detachment gives you freedom. The freedom to think clearly. The freedom to stay consistent. The freedom to go live your life instead of watching your portfolio every hour.

Because the best returns do not come from constant involvement. They come from consistent alignment. With your goals. With your strategy. With your values.

You are not your balance. You are the builder. You are the owner. You are the architect of a long-term system that works, even when the market does not cooperate for a while.

And when you stop giving your self-worth to a number that changes every day, you take back the power that truly builds wealth.

The power to stay.

The power to hold.

The power to choose peace over panic.

And that is the real balance worth protecting.

HOW THE WEALTHY STAY CALM IN CHAOS

MENTAL MODELS FOR STAYING THE COURSE

The difference between people who build wealth and people who constantly struggle with money is rarely just about access or education or even luck. It is about orientation. It is about how they see the world when the world becomes unpredictable. Because everyone faces chaos. Everyone faces volatility. Everyone watches their investments drop at some point. But not everyone responds the same way.

The wealthy have a way of staying calm when the world gets noisy. It is not because they have more information. It is not because they are smarter or faster or more connected. It is because they think in systems. They trust their frameworks. And they refuse to let temporary conditions dictate long-term behavior.

This is not a personality trait. It is a mental model. And it can be learned.

The first principle wealthy investors internalize is that volatility is normal. Not just expected. Normal. They do not see a correction as a crisis. They see it as part of the game. Markets move in cycles. Sentiment swings. News breaks. Algorithms react. Prices fall. Prices rise. All of it is movement. And movement is not the enemy. It is the context in which wealth is built.

Because the long-term trend of productive human progress is upward. Not in a straight line. But in a strong direction. As long as technology continues to advance, as long as businesses continue to innovate, as long as demand continues to evolve, the upward motion will continue. The wealthy understand that the short term is unpredictable. But the direction of progress is not.

The second principle is that price and value are not the same.

Most people see a price drop and assume the investment is broken. But price is what you pay. Value is what you own. Wealthy investors do not panic because the market is down. They ask whether the fundamentals have changed. They ask whether the companies they own are still delivering value, still generating cash flow, still leading in their sectors. If the answer is yes, they stay. Sometimes they buy more. But they do not sell just because the screen turns red.

They understand that volatility is the cost of admission. And the returns are worth the price.

The third principle is time arbitrage.

Wealthy investors think in years and decades. Most people think in days and weeks. That difference creates an advantage. When others are panicking because of what might happen next quarter, they are positioning for what will matter next decade. That is time arbitrage. Choosing patience when others choose urgency. Choosing scale when others choose speed. Choosing vision when others choose reaction.

This is how wealth compounds. Not by predicting the next move. But by staying aligned with trends that are already in motion and giving them enough time to work.

The fourth principle is to think in systems, not events.

Most investors focus on moments. They look for signals. They wait for news. They react to headlines. But wealthy investors think in systems. They build structures that operate regardless of short-term events. They automate contributions. They diversify with intention. They hold assets that are built to grow. They do not react to noise. They trust the structure they designed.

This is what makes funds like SMH and QQQ so attractive to strategic investors. These are not bets on events. They are allocations to systems. Systems that represent critical infrastructure. Systems that evolve. Systems that scale. You do not need to predict when artificial intelligence will reach maturity. You need to own the platforms and technologies that will be essential to its growth. You do not need to guess which country will lead the next chip cycle. You need to hold the companies that make that race possible.

The fifth principle is emotional distance.

The wealthy do not attach their identity to market outcomes. They know the market does not owe them anything. They also know that it cannot take anything from them if their strategy is sound. So they do not let emotions drive decisions. They let information guide them. They let clarity steer them. They trust their convictions because they are built on research, not on fear or hype.

They might feel discomfort. But they do not let discomfort dictate behavior.

They create space between the market and their mindset. And in that space, they find calm.

The final principle is that wealth is not about reacting. It is about positioning.

When others react to headlines, the wealthy ask better questions. What will matter five years from now. What assets are still compounding. What systems will become more essential over time. What companies are still reinvesting at high returns. What platforms are gaining share. What infrastructure is becoming more critical.

Then they put their money there. Not once. Consistently. Patiently. Intentionally.

That is what calm looks like. Not detachment. Not indifference. Just discipline in motion.

You do not need millions to think this way. You need the courage to zoom out. You need the wisdom to build a plan and stay with it. You need the awareness to separate emotion from action. You need the commitment to stay invested even when it feels uncomfortable.

Because wealth is not built in moments of comfort. It is built in moments of clarity.

And clarity comes when you stop reacting to the storm and remember the direction you are heading.

Stay calm. Stay aligned. Stay the course.

That is how the wealthy do it. And you can too.

05
BUILDING A BULLETPROOF WEALTH STRATEGY

TURN ETFS INTO A SYSTEM,
NOT JUST A STOCK PICK

MAIN POINTS

» **The Core-Satellite Approach**
How to use SMH and QQQ as the foundation of a portfolio

» **Dollar-Cost Averaging in Action**
Your unfair advantage in volatile markets

» **When to Buy, When to Hold, When to Chill**
A framework for action and inaction

» **Automate Your Wealth Engine**
Systems to make wealth-building frictionless

» **The Exit Plan: What Does Wealth Do For You?**
Reverse-engineering the life you want

» **How to Avoid Over-Optimizing**
Keep it simple, scalable, and sustainable

THE CORE-SATELLITE APPROACH

HOW TO USE SMH AND QQQ AS THE FOUNDATION OF A PORTFOLIO

Most people invest without a strategy. They chase headlines. They listen to hot tips. They jump in and out of positions hoping to catch the next breakout. The result is a scattered portfolio filled with disconnected ideas. Nothing compounds. Nothing scales. And nothing feels certain.

But wealth is not built on scattered moves. It is built on structure. It is built on systems that remove emotion, simplify decisions, and channel your capital toward assets that consistently deliver value. That is where the core-satellite approach comes in.

Think of your portfolio like a solar system. The core is your sun. It is stable. It is central. It powers everything else. The satellites are your planets. They are smaller, more dynamic, and orbit around the core. This structure creates balance. It gives you exposure to opportunity without compromising your foundation.

The core should do most of the heavy lifting. It should be built around assets that are diversified, resilient, and positioned for long-term growth. That is exactly what makes SMH and QQQ ideal candidates for the center of your portfolio.

Start with QQQ. It holds one hundred of the most innovative companies in the world. These are firms with global scale, high margins, and deep economic moats. They represent the engines of the modern economy. Software. Artificial intelligence. Cloud computing. Cybersecurity. Biotech. Digital infrastructure. QQQ captures the essence of scalable growth and distributes your capital across a wide range of companies that are not just leading today but shaping tomorrow.

QQQ becomes the backbone. It is where you place the capital that you want to work steadily and powerfully over time. You do not trade it. You hold it. You contribute to it. You let it build.

Next is SMH. While QQQ gives you broad exposure to the innovation economy, SMH gives you deep exposure to its foundation: Semiconductors. These companies do not just support technology. They make it possible. Every breakthrough in artificial intelligence, robotics, data science, and connectivity depends on the chipmakers, designers, and equipment providers inside SMH. And these are not fringe players. They are mission-critical to national security, global supply chains, and next-generation computing.

SMH becomes your conviction core. It is slightly more concentrated, slightly more volatile, but deeply aligned with the direction of progress. Together, SMH and QQQ form a balanced and future-facing core that gives you access to both the infrastructure and the application layers of the digital economy.

Now that your core is in place, the satellite positions can serve a very different purpose.

Satellites are where you can add specific themes, industries, or ideas that reflect your individual point of view. Maybe you believe clean energy will accelerate. Maybe you want exposure to emerging markets. Maybe you want to hold a few individual stocks you understand deeply. These can orbit your core. But they should never replace it.

Your core gives you peace of mind. Your satellites give you flexibility.

This structure also helps with risk management. If a satellite underperforms, it does not threaten your financial future. If the core continues to perform, your wealth continues to grow. You avoid overexposure to any single story. You stay grounded in systems that have already proven their value.

The beauty of the core-satellite model is that it adapts as you grow. Early on, your satellites might be small. Your capital is focused. Your contributions are building mass. As your portfolio grows, you can allocate more to ideas you care about. You can explore niches. You can take calculated risks. But the core stays the same. It stays consistent. It stays strong.

And that consistency gives you a massive psychological edge. You are not wondering what to do every time the market moves. You are not trying to outthink every headline. You have already made the most important decision. You are investing in systems, not stories. You are building with conviction, not reacting with confusion.

This model also aligns beautifully with long-term goals. If you want to retire early, if you want to fund a business, if you want to create intergenerational wealth, you need stability and growth. You need assets that are built to last. You need investments that reflect the structure of the future, not the traditions of the past.

SMH and QQQ are not just ETFs. They are signals. They say you believe in innovation. You believe in ownership. You believe in long-term compounding. You believe in building wealth with intention, not luck.

With this foundation in place, the rest of your strategy becomes easier. You can automate your contributions. You can rebalance with clarity. You can tune out the noise and stay focused on what actually moves the needle.

Because once you stop treating investing like a series of random picks and start treating it like a system, everything changes.

And it all begins with what you choose to place at the center.

DOLLAR-COST AVERAGING IN ACTION

YOUR UNFAIR ADVANTAGE IN VOLATILE MARKETS

Timing the market feels like power. Precision. Control. The idea that you can jump in right before prices rise and get out right before they fall is intoxicating. But it rarely works. Even professional investors struggle to time the market consistently. The data shows that most individual investors underperform the very assets they invest in, not because the assets are flawed, but because their behavior is.

That is where dollar-cost averaging comes in. It removes the pressure of perfect timing and replaces it with something more powerful. A system. A rhythm. A structure that transforms volatility from a threat into a tool.

Dollar-cost averaging is the practice of investing a fixed amount of money at regular intervals, regardless of market conditions. Whether the market is up or down, you invest the same amount. Over time, this strategy automatically buys more shares when prices are low and fewer when prices are high. Without trying to predict the market, you are automatically reducing your average cost per share and building a position that reflects the real shape of long-term opportunity.

It sounds simple. And it is. But do not mistake simplicity for weakness. Dollar-cost averaging is one of the most psychologically resilient and mathematically consistent approaches to investing ever created.

When markets fall, most investors panic. They hesitate. They wait for clarity. They wait for a bottom that never announces itself. But the investor who uses dollar-cost averaging stays calm. They know that lower prices mean greater accumulation. They do not need to guess when to act. Their system acts for them. Their capital keeps working. Their discipline compounds.

When markets rise, most investors chase. They feel late. They feel like they missed the opportunity. So they rush in, often at elevated prices. But the dollar-cost averaging investor has already been building their position. They are not reacting. They are participating. And their position continues to grow in value without drama.

This strategy is especially powerful when paired with funds like SMH and QQQ. These are not speculative assets. They are engines of innovation and long-term value creation. When you buy them regularly over time, you are not just averaging your cost. You are anchoring your portfolio in sectors that continue to grow, adapt, and lead.

Think about what happens when you commit to a monthly investment into QQQ. Each month, regardless of headlines, you add to your ownership of companies like Apple, Microsoft, Amazon, and NVIDIA. You are not waiting for confirmation. You are not reacting to earnings reports. You are allocating to global platforms that scale, monetize, and compound. Month after month. Year after year.

Do the same with SMH and you gain deep exposure to semiconductor companies that are essential to every modern industry. These companies are cyclical in the short term but foundational in the long term. As the world becomes more connected, more intelligent, and more automated, the demand for semiconductors will only rise. By dollar-cost averaging into SMH, you gain increasing ownership in that future regardless of market sentiment.

This method is not about being passive. It is about being intentional. You are not ignoring the market. You are choosing not to dance with its mood swings. You are aligning your contributions with your convictions. You are letting time, not emotion, drive your behavior.

And the beauty is that this strategy scales. Whether you are investing one hundred dollars a month or ten thousand, the principle remains the same. Steady contribution. Automatic execution. Emotional detachment. Strategic accumulation.

You can automate it through your broker. You can set reminders if you prefer manual control. The important thing is not how you do it. The important thing is that you keep doing it.

Dollar-cost averaging turns time into your ally. It makes volatility your friend. It converts hesitation into habit. And it builds wealth not through speed, but through consistency.

It also protects you from one of the most dangerous investing behaviors: Waiting. Waiting for a dip. Waiting for confirmation. Waiting until you feel ready. The investor who waits is always one step behind. The investor who acts consistently is always one step ahead.

Because investing is not about having perfect timing. It is about having a repeatable process that puts your capital in motion.

Dollar-cost averaging is that process. It removes the guesswork. It removes the guilt. It removes the paralysis.

And it builds.

Slowly. Silently. Powerfully.

So the next time the market feels uncertain, remember this. You do not need to predict what happens next.

You need to keep showing up. Keep allocating. Keep building.

Because the future does not reward perfect entry. It rewards consistent presence.

WHEN TO BUY, WHEN TO HOLD, WHEN TO CHILL

A FRAMEWORK FOR ACTION AND INACTION

Most investors are always looking for something to do. Some new move to make. A stock to buy. A signal to follow. A trade to execute. They equate activity with intelligence. They believe motion equals progress. But great investing is often the opposite. It is knowing when to act with urgency and when to sit in stillness. It is knowing that inaction is not a lack of discipline. It is the presence of it.

The market will always tempt you with reasons to act. News. Charts. Rumors. Trends. There will always be something moving and someone saying you are missing out. But the difference between reactive investors and strategic builders is not just what they do. It is when they do it. Timing matters. But not the kind you hear about on financial news.

The timing that matters is emotional timing. The ability to act from clarity, not fear. The ability to step back when others are rushing in. The ability to hold through discomfort and let your strategy unfold.

This is where a simple decision framework becomes powerful. A way to step out of noise and into structure. Think in three clear modes. Buy. Hold. Chill.

WHEN TO BUY

You buy when your system tells you to. Not your emotions. Not your gut. Your system.

If you are using dollar-cost averaging, that means buying at regular intervals. Whether the market is up or down, you buy because that is what your plan says. If you are adding to your portfolio because your income increased or you freed up capital, you buy because you have conviction in the assets you are building around.

You buy when the market drops and you see value where others see fear. You buy when your core assets, like SMH and QQQ, are temporarily mispriced compared to their long-term potential. You buy not to chase momentum, but to strengthen your foundation.

Buying is not a reaction. It is an allocation of belief. You are choosing to place capital in systems that reflect your vision of the future. You are expanding ownership of infrastructure that you understand, respect, and trust.

WHEN TO HOLD

You hold when you are already positioned correctly.

Holding is not passive. It is a choice. It is the decision to let compounding do its work. It is the ability to watch a great asset grow without touching it, adjusting it, or second-guessing it. It is the patience to let time create the results your strategy is designed to deliver.

You hold through volatility. You hold through sideways markets. You hold even when others are trying to convince you that some new asset or strategy will work faster.

The truth is that most wealth is lost not by poor purchases, but by premature exits. Investors sell too early. They get spooked. They want to rotate. They want to take profits. But in trying to capture short-term gains, they miss the long-term miracle.

When you own companies through QQQ that are redefining how the world operates, or when you hold SMH because you believe semiconductors will continue powering the next generation of progress, you do not need constant action. You need intelligent patience.

WHEN TO CHILL

You chill when nothing is broken. When your plan is working. When your allocations reflect your priorities. You chill when the market is loud, but your conviction is louder. You chill when everything in you wants to check your portfolio for the fifth time today, but you remember that your real edge is not found in more updates, it is found in fewer reactions.

Chilling is an underrated financial skill.

It requires confidence. It requires detachment from noise. It requires maturity to know that movement is not always necessary. It is what keeps you grounded when everyone else is spinning. It is what keeps your capital growing while others are panicking.

You chill when the media is screaming recession. You chill when social media is pushing hype. You chill when volatility makes others question their plans. Not because you do not care. But because you already built your plan to survive exactly these conditions.

That calm is your edge. That stillness is your strength.

So when the market falls, do not assume you need to change everything. Ask first: Should I be buying more, or should I be holding firm. And if the answer is neither, then do the most powerful thing you can do.

Chill.

Let the work you already did continue working.

Let the capital you already placed continue compounding.

Let the future you already aligned with continue unfolding.

A strategy that tells you when to act is good. A strategy that also tells you when not to is even better.

Because the investors who win are not the ones who do the most.

They are the ones who do the right things at the right time, and have the clarity to do nothing when nothing needs to be done.

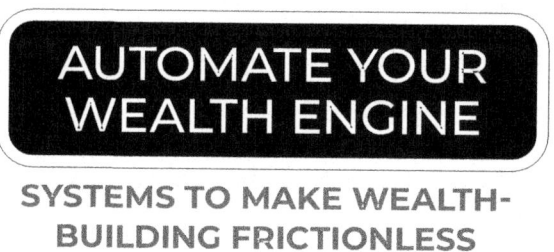

AUTOMATE YOUR WEALTH ENGINE

SYSTEMS TO MAKE WEALTH-BUILDING FRICTIONLESS

Most people believe wealth is built through willpower. Stay disciplined. Stay focused. Show up every day. While there is truth in that mindset, it ignores a more powerful and sustainable path: Automation.

Wealth is not just about working hard or making the right picks. It is about building a system that removes decision fatigue, reduces emotional interference, and creates momentum that does not depend on your mood, your motivation, or your memory.

The most successful investors do not rely on constant effort. They rely on automated infrastructure. They understand that consistency outperforms intensity. And automation is the highest form of consistency.

Automation begins with your contributions. The moment you automate a recurring transfer from your income to your investment account, you create leverage. You eliminate the need to think about it. You bypass hesitation. You stop negotiating with yourself every month. The decision is made once. The system repeats it forever.

Whether it is one hundred dollars or ten thousand, the act of automatic investing transforms your savings into a living engine. Each month, that engine grows stronger. It compounds faster. It moves forward even when you are distracted, overwhelmed, or discouraged.

You can automate through your brokerage. Set a monthly buy into QQQ or SMH. Let the money flow from your bank account, get invested immediately, and sit quietly compounding while you focus on building your life. No confirmation needed. No emotion involved. Just forward motion.

The next layer of automation is rebalancing.

As your portfolio grows, some positions will outperform. Others will lag. Your original allocation may begin to drift. Left unchecked, that drift can expose you to more risk than intended. Or cause you to miss out on opportunities that no longer align with your plan.

You can automate rebalancing quarterly or annually. Most brokerages offer this service. If not, set a calendar reminder and rebalance manually. The goal is not to tweak constantly. The goal is to maintain strategic alignment without emotional interference.

Another powerful form of automation is dividend reinvestment.

Many of the companies within QQQ and SMH pay dividends. You can choose to take those dividends as cash or reinvest them back into the fund. Reinvestment is automation in its purest form. It takes the return generated by your portfolio and puts it back to work immediately. No waiting. No analysis. Just compounding.

This is how wealth multiplies. Not just from your original contributions. But from the capital your capital creates. The faster you put that return back into motion, the more exponential your growth becomes.

Beyond the technical mechanics, automation protects your psychology.

The market will tempt you to act when action is not needed. It will trigger fear when you should be holding. It will create urgency when patience is the right call. Automation cuts through that noise. It gives you a reason to stay still. It reinforces discipline without willpower. It creates a plan that works even when your emotions do not.

It also frees your time and energy to focus on things that actually move the needle. You are no longer spending hours researching market trends, checking your phone during meetings, second-guessing your contributions. You are simply living your life while your system builds your future in the background.

And that is the real power of automation. Not just efficiency. Not just consistency. Peace.

You no longer carry the weight of daily decisions. You no longer need to be perfect. You no longer need to win every time. Your system does not chase. It builds.

This is how high-performing people protect their attention. They automate what does not need their creativity. They focus on their work, their families, their purpose. Meanwhile, their money is working. Their wealth is growing. Their freedom is compounding.

You do not need to reinvent the process every month. You need to set it up once, then step back and trust it.

Set your contributions. Automate your buys. Reinvest your returns. Rebalance periodically. Keep it simple. Keep it consistent.

That is your wealth engine.

And once it is running, the most powerful thing you can do is stay out of its way.

THE EXIT PLAN – WHAT DOES WEALTH DO FOR YOU

REVERSE-ENGINEERING THE LIFE YOU WANT

Most people focus their entire financial life on accumulation. Grow the portfolio. Maximize returns. Watch the number rise. But very few ever stop to ask the more important question.

What is all of this for.

What does wealth actually enable. What does it give you beyond numbers. Beyond status. Beyond the feeling of safety. Because unless you define the purpose of your wealth, you risk spending your entire life climbing a ladder that leads nowhere.

This is where the exit plan begins. Not with the market. Not with asset allocation. But with clarity. The clarity to define your version of enough. Your version of freedom. Your version of a well-lived life.

Wealth is not the destination. It is the engine. And if you do not decide where you are going, you will spend your life in motion without ever feeling progress.

So take a step back and ask with honesty and specificity. What kind of life do I want my money to make possible. What do I want more of. What do I want less of. What would I do if money were not a limiting factor.

Maybe you want to retire early and spend more time with your family. Maybe you want to travel without checking prices. Maybe you want to start a business, fund a nonprofit, support a cause, or simply buy your time back from the calendar. Whatever it is, you need to name it. Because once you do, you can work backward.

Your exit plan begins with your vision. Then it maps that vision onto financial reality.

How much would that life cost per year. How much passive income would you need to sustain it. What would your portfolio need to generate in order to support that income. What level of risk are you willing to accept to reach that number. How many years do you have before you want that life to begin.

This is not fantasy. This is design. And once you run the numbers, something powerful happens. Your portfolio stops being abstract. It becomes personal. It becomes directional. You are no longer investing for the sake of growth alone. You are investing to create something real.

Now you can align your strategy.

If your goal is to live off your portfolio, you may want to build toward a combination of growth and income. SMH and QQQ provide that growth, especially in the early stages. They give you exposure to sectors that are driving productivity, innovation, and global economic expansion. As your portfolio matures, you might shift a portion into assets that generate yield. But the core remains. Because even in retirement, you want your capital to keep working.

Your contributions now have purpose. Your automation has a destination. You are no longer asking whether the market is up or down this week. You are asking whether your system is getting you closer to the life you designed.

Your exit plan also helps you stay grounded when the market turns. Because you are not investing for ego. You are investing for freedom. You are not playing the game to beat someone else. You are playing to win your own version of life. That clarity builds resilience. It removes the pressure to be perfect. It gives you the space to stay invested even when conditions are tough.

And it reminds you that you do not need infinite money. You need aligned money. You do not need to chase every opportunity. You need to own the opportunities that matter for your goals.

Think of your portfolio as a machine. But you are the architect. You decide what it builds. You decide when it is enough. You decide how and when to step off the treadmill and start living.

The exit is not the end. It is the transition. From growth to freedom. From chasing to owning. From building to enjoying.

And that transition does not need to be a cliff. It can be a glide path. You can reduce hours. You can build in sabbaticals. You can test versions of the life you want long before you hit your full number. The earlier you define your vision, the earlier you can start designing your way into it.

That is what wealth is for. Not just accumulation. Activation.

So ask the question. What does wealth allow me to do that I cannot do today. What kind of life do I want to wake up into five years from now. What investments give me the highest probability of funding that life.

The moment you answer those questions, your portfolio becomes more than a collection of assets.

It becomes your blueprint.

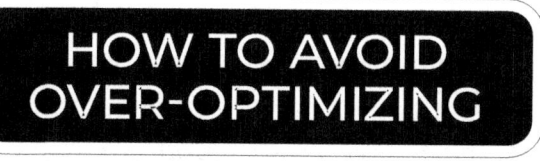

HOW TO AVOID OVER-OPTIMIZING

KEEP IT SIMPLE, SCALABLE, AND SUSTAINABLE

The modern investor has unlimited tools. Real-time data. Endless news. Infinite options. You can check your portfolio in the grocery store, trade from your phone while walking into a meeting, or rebalance from the beach. Information is instant. Markets are global. Access is frictionless.

And with that power comes a hidden danger: Over-optimization.

The temptation to tweak is constant. Maybe you should change your allocation. Maybe that sector is heating up. Maybe this new fund has slightly better expense ratios. Maybe this model performs better in downturns. The voice of over-optimization does not shout. It whispers. Just make this one small change. Just adjust this one setting. Just check one more chart.

But small changes made constantly create big problems. They erode consistency. They interrupt compounding. They drain your focus. They make you question systems that were never broken to begin with. In the pursuit of better, you lose what is already working.

The truth is that most investors do not fail from bad strategy. They fail from abandoned strategy. They build something smart, then get bored. They want more excitement. They chase upgrades. They listen to louder voices. They forget that simplicity scales. They forget that the system only works if you let it work.

Wealth does not come from perfecting every input. It comes from holding steady over time.

The investors who win are not the ones who optimize everything. They are the ones who commit to the few things that matter and repeat them with discipline. They automate their contributions. They invest in quality. They let go of the need to predict. They measure progress in years, not weeks.

This is why building your portfolio around SMH and QQQ is so powerful. These funds already give you exposure to the highest-leverage parts of the economy. You own the platforms and the infrastructure. You own the drivers of growth and the enablers of innovation. You do not need to outguess them. You need to stay invested in them.

If you start with a clear system, automatic contributions, diversified across scalable growth assets, with periodic rebalancing, you already have ninety percent of what you need. Chasing the remaining ten percent of optimization often causes more harm than good.

That is because most optimization is driven by fear. Fear of underperformance. Fear of missing out. Fear that someone else has found a better formula. But optimization built on fear does not lead to better outcomes. It leads to more noise. It leads to more second-guessing. It leads to complexity that breaks under pressure.

Simplicity is not laziness. Simplicity is design. Simplicity is intelligence in motion.

When your wealth strategy is simple, it is teachable. You can explain it to your family. You can pass it on to your children. You can stay with it when life gets busy, when markets get noisy, or when your attention is pulled elsewhere. Simplicity is what makes your strategy sustainable.

And sustainability is the most important quality any system can have.

You do not need to outperform every year. You need to stay in the game for decades. You do not need to tweak your allocation every month. You need to contribute through every market cycle. You do not need to optimize every percentage point. You need to own the future and hold it long enough for the future to pay you back.

When you feel the urge to optimize, pause. Ask whether the change improves clarity or just creates motion. Ask whether the change supports your vision or just feeds your anxiety. Ask whether the system you already built is broken or just boring.

Because wealth creation is often boring, and that is exactly what makes it work.

Let others chase complexity. Let others scramble for the next upgrade. You have a system that works. You have assets that compound. You have automation that removes friction. You have alignment between your capital and your convictions.

That is more than enough.

Let your portfolio be a place of calm. Let your plan be a source of strength. Let your strategy be the quiet background to a bold, free, and meaningful life.

And let simplicity be your edge.

Because in a world obsessed with more, clarity is rare. And clarity builds wealth.

06
WHAT THE MARKET DOESN'T SAY OUT LOUD

INSIDER TRUTHS THE MEDIA WON'T TELL YOU, BUT YOUR PORTFOLIO NEEDS TO KNOW

MAIN POINTS

» Volatility ≠ Risk
Why daily price swings are noise, not danger

» Corrections Are Gifts
How market dips become wealth accelerators

» Media Panic is Market Fuel
How headlines manipulate emotion, not data

» Wall Street Wants You Confused
The incentive behind complexity

» What Real Risk Looks Like
The hidden danger of not investing

» The Boring Truth About Wealth
Why the best returns are often the least exciting

VOLATILITY ≠ RISK

WHY DAILY PRICE SWINGS ARE NOISE, NOT DANGER

There is a word that terrifies new investors. It pops up in headlines. It flashes red on screens. It sends people running to cash, delaying decisions, doubting their strategy.

That word is volatility.

And it is almost always misunderstood.

Volatility is not risk. But most people treat it that way. They open their portfolio, see the numbers jump or fall, and immediately feel exposed. They watch a fund drop three percent in a single day and assume something is broken. They feel like they need to act. They worry that if they do not act, they will lose everything.

But volatility is not danger. It is movement. It is noise. It is the natural rhythm of a market that is constantly adjusting, reacting, recalibrating. It is the price of liquidity. It is the reflection of emotion. It is how the market breathes.

If you confuse volatility with risk, you will sabotage your own growth. You will exit when you should be holding. You will hesitate when you should be buying. You will spend your energy managing your emotions instead of managing your plan.

Risk is the chance of permanent loss. Volatility is the experience of temporary discomfort.

Those two things are not the same.

The companies inside funds like SMH and QQQ are not fragile. They do not vanish because the market had a red week. These are firms with global footprints, strong cash flow, pricing power, and long-term demand. Their stock prices may fluctuate, but their value creation continues. Their innovation does not pause just because investors got nervous for a few days.

Volatility often tells you more about investor psychology than company performance.

Look at any chart of QQQ over the past twenty years. You will see dips. Some of them sharp. You will see moments when fear ruled the market. But if you kept holding, you saw the curve bend upward. Because the businesses inside the fund kept building. They kept scaling. They kept compounding.

Volatility is not a sign that something is wrong. It is a feature of an open market. It is the mechanism through which assets find new owners. Every time a share is sold in panic, it is bought in conviction. Every price move is a reflection of someone stepping away and someone else stepping in.

If you are the one stepping in when others step back, volatility becomes your advantage.

This is how professional investors see it. They do not fear volatility. They use it. They understand that it is often the best time to accumulate positions. They look for moments when the price of an asset disconnects from its long-term value. They step in while others wait for reassurance. That is how wealth is transferred.

The problem is that retail investors are taught to be afraid of red. They are taught to avoid discomfort. They are trained to think like speculators, not owners. But volatility only hurts when you are unsure of what you own. When you understand your holdings, when you believe in the long-term thesis, volatility becomes background noise.

That is why clarity matters more than prediction.

If you know why you own something, you do not need to explain every movement. You do not need to track every headline. You do not need to watch every price update. You hold because you understand. You hold because your assets are aligned with the future, not with the mood of the moment.

SMH and QQQ are built for that kind of holding. They are not speculative bets. They are curated portfolios of market-leading companies in sectors that are structurally positioned for growth. They are designed to give you exposure to the most productive engines of the global economy. Not just this quarter, but for years to come.

They will fluctuate. That is guaranteed. But the fluctuation is not failure. It is flow.

The goal of investing is not to eliminate volatility. It is to navigate it without losing conviction.

That requires a new lens.

Instead of asking how do I avoid volatility, ask how do I stay committed through it.

Instead of asking when will the market calm down, ask how can I make volatility irrelevant to my plan.

Instead of asking what if this drops more, ask what will this be worth in ten years.

Volatility does not destroy wealth. Reaction to it does.

Every long-term investor has lived through dozens of dips. Every successful portfolio has weathered fear, uncertainty, and sharp declines. The ones that endure are the ones that are rooted in a strategy, not swayed by emotion.

Volatility will not go away. But your response to it can change.

You can stop flinching at red. You can stop chasing green. You can stop trying to time the un-timable.

And you can start treating volatility for what it really is.

Not a warning. Not a verdict. Just movement.

And movement is not the enemy. In fact, it is often the invitation.

CORRECTIONS ARE GIFTS

HOW MARKET DIPS BECOME WEALTH ACCELERATORS

Every investor says they want to buy low and sell high. It sounds obvious. It sounds wise. But when prices actually fall, when red floods the screen, when uncertainty takes over, very few follow through. The same people who say they want a discount suddenly want out. They retreat. They freeze. They wait for the storm to pass.

And they miss the moment they claimed to be waiting for.

This is the paradox of market corrections. Everyone wants the upside of buying the dip. But few are prepared for the emotional cost of doing it. The fear. The doubt. The second-guessing. And yet those who step in when others pull back are often the ones who build the strongest long-term returns.

Because corrections are not catastrophes. They are gifts.

A correction is a broad market decline of ten percent or more from recent highs. It is a normal part of market behavior. It happens regularly. It reflects recalibration, not collapse. And while it can feel painful in the moment, it is often one of the most strategic entry points you will ever see.

Think about what happens during a correction. Great companies go on sale. Their products still sell. Their margins remain healthy. Their growth engines keep running. But their stock price falls because fear spreads faster than facts. The asset becomes temporarily mispriced. Not because the business is broken, but because investors are emotional.

That gap between price and value is where opportunity lives.

If you are holding cash or allocating consistently, corrections are accelerators. They allow you to buy more ownership in future-facing companies at a lower cost. And when the market recovers, as it has after every correction in modern history, you do not just participate. You benefit disproportionately.

This is not theory. It is backed by data.

Most of the market's strongest days follow directly after a correction. Investors who stay out miss not just the bottom, but the early bounce. They miss the gains that often make up a huge portion of annual returns. And those missed days are almost impossible to recover.

Corrections also serve another purpose. They clean the system. They wash out speculation. They humble overconfidence. They create space for strong hands to step in. They allow capital to rotate back into companies that actually matter, those with real value, real leadership, and real alignment with the future.

This is exactly where funds like SMH and QQQ shine. These are not fragile positions. They represent durable companies in sectors that drive global productivity. Technology. Semiconductors. Artificial intelligence. Cloud computing. Digital infrastructure. These are not just themes. They are foundations. When their prices fall during a correction, the underlying value remains strong. And that disconnect becomes your invitation.

Corrections are not the time to run. They are the time to remember what you own. They are the time to re-read your thesis. They are the time to act, not out of emotion, but out of clarity.

This requires courage. Not reckless boldness. Quiet courage. The courage to zoom out. The courage to trust your plan. The courage to see falling prices not as failure, but as friction on the way to freedom.

It also requires structure.

Having an automated contribution schedule helps. Having cash set aside for opportunistic investing helps. Having conviction in your holdings helps. These things do not eliminate fear. They make it manageable. They give you a system that can operate even when your emotions do not want to cooperate.

Corrections are also a psychological test. They reveal who is playing games and who is building wealth. They show who has a strategy and who is improvising. They expose the difference between ownership and speculation.

The people who panic are often those who never truly believed in their investments. The people who stay calm, and even lean in, are those who understood what they owned before the market fell.

That is why preparation matters more than prediction.

You do not need to know when the next correction will happen. You need to be structurally ready for it. Emotionally ready for it. Strategically ready to treat it not as a crisis, but as a window.

Because corrections are temporary. But the decisions you make during them can echo for decades.

Do not fear the red. Study it. Use it. Let it serve you.

Because when the world goes on sale, wealth builders do not walk away.

They walk in.

MEDIA PANIC IS MARKET FUEL
HOW HEADLINES MANIPULATE EMOTION, NOT DATA

Turn on any financial news outlet during a market downturn and you will see flashing red graphics, bold letters announcing market chaos, experts predicting recession, and talking heads debating whether the system is about to break. The tone is urgent. The music is dramatic. The mood is unmistakable.

Panic sells.

Because panic grabs attention. Panic drives clicks. Panic keeps you tuned in through the commercial break. And in an age where every outlet competes for your eyes, attention has become currency. The more dramatic the story, the more valuable it is to the platform telling it.

But the stories that capture attention rarely support sound decision-making. In fact, they often lead you away from the actions that build wealth. Media is not designed to help you invest wisely. It is designed to keep you watching.

This creates a dangerous feedback loop.

The media amplifies fear. Investors respond by selling or freezing. The market dips. The headlines intensify. More investors react. More red appears on the screen. The fear grows stronger. The story feeds itself.

But the story is not the reality. It is a lens. A filter. One that distorts the long-term trajectory of the market by zooming in on every bump, every whisper, every what-if scenario that can be dramatized into a segment.

The truth is that most headlines are not designed to tell you what is happening. They are designed to make you feel something about what is happening. Uncertainty. Urgency. Outrage. Envy. That is not information. That is manipulation.

Understanding this changes everything.

You stop reacting to headlines and start questioning them. You stop asking what the news says and start asking what the data shows. You stop living in twelve-hour cycles and start thinking in twelve-year timeframes.

And you begin to realize something powerful. Media panic often signals market opportunity.

When fear hits the front page, it usually means prices have already dropped. When everyone is asking if it is the end, it often means we are closer to the bottom than the top. When financial experts start sounding like doomsday prophets, that is when the best investors start placing new capital.

Because smart capital does not wait for calm. It waits for dislocation. Dislocation between price and value. Dislocation between perception and fundamentals. Dislocation between noise and signal.

The companies inside QQQ and SMH do not become worthless because a headline says tech is falling. They do not stop innovating because a host declares it is time to be fearful. These are long-term growth machines. Their relevance does not vanish in a week. Their infrastructure does not disappear in a month.

The media may suggest that the world is ending. But inside these companies, engineers are still solving problems. Customers are still using products. Data is still being processed. Chips are still being built. Revenue is still being generated. Innovation is still compounding.

And investors who understand that reality stay calm while others spin out.

This is not about ignoring news. It is about filtering it. It is about training yourself to distinguish between stories that sell fear and signals that guide action. It is about remembering that the market moves on sentiment in the short term and on fundamentals in the long term.

The key is to anchor your thinking in what you own, not in what they say.

When you own companies with pricing power, durable moats, scalable products, and world-class talent, you do not need media permission to hold. You do not need reassurance from headlines to feel conviction. You have your own framework. Your own research. Your own plan.

That plan should not swing with the news cycle. It should reflect your belief in progress, in compounding, in systems that get stronger over time. QQQ and SMH are filled with companies that represent that kind of system. They are not media narratives. They are business engines.

And those engines keep running while the headlines scream.

So the next time you see panic across your screen, pause. Breathe. Zoom out.

Ask yourself if the story reflects data or just drama. Ask if anything about your long-term thesis has actually changed. Ask if this fear is presenting a window instead of a warning.

Because when media panic dominates the airwaves, smart investors do not retreat.

They refocus. They rebalance. Sometimes, they reload.

But they do not run.

They remember that the media sells drama. And wealth is built in the quiet that follows it.

THE INCENTIVE BEHIND COMPLEXITY

There is a quiet truth that most investors never hear. Simplicity works. But simplicity does not sell. And that is why Wall Street rarely speaks it out loud.

The financial industry thrives on complexity. It packages it. Brands it. Markets it. It creates products with long names, charts that look like blueprints for a spaceship, and strategies that promise to outperform through precision, timing, and innovation. These products are wrapped in language that feels elite. They speak in acronyms, reference models, and project confidence that borders on mysticism.

And most investors, feeling out of their depth, defer.

They assume they are not supposed to understand. They assume wealth building is only for those who speak the language. They assume complexity equals intelligence and trust the system that looks the most complicated.

But that assumption is exactly what the system depends on.

Because confusion keeps you dependent. It keeps you hiring layers of managers, paying unnecessary fees, bouncing from fund to fund, advisor to advisor, strategy to strategy. Every time you feel like you are not doing enough or not doing it right, someone is waiting to sell you the next best thing. Confusion is not a byproduct of the system. It is part of the business model.

That is why clarity is so rare. And so powerful.

When you understand that most of what passes for financial advice is engineered complexity, you can begin to strip away the noise. You can begin to see that true wealth building does not require secret knowledge or access to exclusive products. It requires ownership of productive assets, consistent contributions, and the ability to stay the course when others panic.

The companies inside QQQ and SMH do not need complicated wrappers to deliver value. They are businesses with real customers, real cash flow, and real impact on the global economy. Their power is not hidden in strategy. It is visible in scale. When you invest in them, you are not just accessing an asset class. You are buying a stake in systems that power modern life.

But Wall Street rarely promotes that message. Because it is not as profitable.

It is more profitable to build a product with layers of hedging, options, derivatives, and leverage, then charge you to access it, and charge you again to manage it. It is more profitable to promise downside protection through high-fee vehicles that underperform in calm markets and collapse in chaos. It is more profitable to keep you chasing.

And yet, when you look at the actual portfolios of the wealthiest families and institutions, the story is very different.

The foundations. The endowments. The sovereign wealth funds. The pensions. They are not trading options all day. They are not buying exotic products on margin. They are allocating to world-class businesses, rebalancing periodically, and staying invested over decades. They are not looking for magic. They are looking for consistency.

They understand that real wealth is built on focus, not flair.

So why is it so hard for individuals to do the same. Because most are never taught that simplicity is an option. They are taught to fear it. To associate it with missed opportunity. To believe that a portfolio built on just a few core positions is too basic, too vulnerable, too plain.

But basic is often beautiful. Plain is often powerful. Vulnerability is often imagined.

A portfolio built around QQQ and SMH is not simplistic. It is strategic. It is direct exposure to innovation, infrastructure, scalability, and the backbone of the digital economy. It is what many complex products are trying to simulate, just with higher fees, more friction, and less transparency.

The investor who sees through the illusion can do something rare. They can build without relying on permission. They can say no to layers. No to confusion. No to the illusion that success must look complicated to be real.

And once they say no to confusion, they are free to say yes to ownership.

Ownership of a strategy they understand. Ownership of assets they believe in. Ownership of a future they can describe without using financial jargon.

You do not need to keep optimizing your plan every quarter. You need to stick to a system that already works. You do not need five advisors giving you conflicting opinions. You need one core philosophy you trust enough to follow through.

Because the truth is this. Wall Street needs you to feel unsure.

But wealth does not.

Wealth needs you to be clear. Aligned. Committed.

And once you choose clarity, you cannot be manipulated.

You become what the system was never built to expect.

A confident investor who no longer needs it.

WHAT REAL RISK LOOKS LIKE

THE HIDDEN DANGER OF NOT INVESTING

Ask most people what they fear about investing and they will tell you the same thing. They are afraid of losing money. They are afraid the market will crash. They are afraid to buy in and then watch prices fall. Their definition of risk is tied to one thing: Volatility.

But volatility is not the enemy. And short-term losses are not the real danger.

The real risk is something much quieter. Much slower. Much easier to ignore until it is too late.

The real risk is not investing at all.

It is watching your money sit still while the cost of life keeps rising. It is holding cash in a savings account that earns less than inflation. It is spending decades in a career while never letting your capital work alongside you. It is missing out on compounding because you wanted certainty instead of strategy.

The market might dip ten percent in a bad month. But inflation quietly takes two or three percent every year without headlines, without drama, without warning. And unlike market losses, which often reverse, inflation is permanent. Once that purchasing power is gone, it does not come back.

Over a decade, the cost of sitting in cash can exceed twenty percent of your wealth. Over two decades, that number becomes exponential. It is not loud. It is not visible. But it compounds. And that silent erosion is one of the greatest financial threats people face.

It gets worse when you consider opportunity cost.

Every year you delay investing, you miss another full year of potential growth. You miss dividend payments. You miss price appreciation. You miss the most valuable component of wealth creation: Time. Time is the one variable you cannot replace. And the longer you wait to invest, the more ground you must cover later just to catch up.

This is why trying to avoid risk by not investing is actually the riskiest move of all.

You are not avoiding volatility. You are guaranteeing stagnation. You are not protecting your capital. You are stranding it. You are not preserving freedom. You are postponing it indefinitely.

Meanwhile, the market keeps moving.

Technology keeps advancing. Companies keep compounding. Assets keep growing. Other people keep building.

And the window you are waiting for keeps closing.

This is not about shaming fear. Fear is human. It is natural to hesitate when your money is on the line. But fear should not be your strategy. It should be your signal to seek clarity, not your reason to stand still.

Because you do not need to be reckless. You need to be positioned.

You do not need to chase every opportunity. You need to own the right ones for long enough to let them work.

Funds like SMH and QQQ are built for exactly this purpose. They give you access to industries that are not just growing but defining the future. Semiconductors. Artificial intelligence. Cloud infrastructure. Scalable software. These are not speculative themes. They are the foundation of the global economy. The longer you wait to participate in them, the more value you leave behind.

The market will rise and fall. But the trend of innovation continues.

And the investor who understands what real risk looks like will not wait for the perfect time to enter. They will understand that the perfect time is yesterday. And the second best time is right now.

Real risk is not about what happens on a bad day. It is about what you lose by not showing up for the next decade.

It is not about a portfolio drop. It is about a life delayed. A retirement deferred. A freedom never claimed because fear kept your money idle and your momentum stuck.

And here is what the market does not say out loud. You can recover from almost any mistake in investing. But you cannot recover from never starting.

That is the one move the market will never reward.

Because wealth belongs to the present. To those who act. To those who allocate. To those who understand that risk is not in volatility.

Risk is in regret.

WHY THE BEST RETURNS ARE OFTEN THE LEAST EXCITING

When people imagine wealth, they picture drama. Huge wins. Sudden breakthroughs. Overnight success. The story of a bold trade that changed everything. A startup that exploded. A coin that multiplied. A moment that made it all happen.

But real wealth does not work like that.

The truth is much more boring.

Real wealth grows slowly. It compounds quietly. It works in the background while you live your life. It does not show up as a headline. It shows up as peace. As freedom. As the ability to choose how you spend your time without asking permission.

But most people miss it because it does not feel exciting. It feels repetitive. Steady. Simple.

It feels like putting a fixed amount into QQQ or SMH every month. It feels like checking your account quarterly instead of hourly. It feels like saying no to shiny distractions and yes to systems that actually work.

It feels like knowing your plan is working even when the market is not.

That kind of investing does not give you adrenaline. It gives you options. It gives you the ability to walk away from jobs you no longer love, to spend time with people who matter, to fund ideas that would otherwise stay stuck inside your imagination.

But to reach that level of freedom, you must learn to fall in love with boring.

You must understand that the most powerful strategy is not hidden in complexity. It is sitting in front of you. Simplicity. Consistency. Time.

Not just time in the market, but time spent staying with the same plan long enough for it to bear fruit. Time spent ignoring noise. Time spent refining habits instead of chasing predictions.

The financial world is filled with distractions. A new strategy. A new platform. A new fund that promises slightly better returns. You can spend your life switching from one to the next, always optimizing, never compounding.

Or you can commit.

You can automate your contributions. You can build around a small number of high-quality assets. You can stay invested through fear and fatigue. You can choose structure over stimulation.

And that structure, as boring as it may seem, becomes your fortress.

It protects your energy. It removes friction. It frees your mind to focus on what matters most.

Because the people who build serious wealth are rarely the loudest in the room. They are not glued to their screens. They are not addicted to the rush of winning a bet. They are calm. Focused. Aligned with something greater than themselves.

Their portfolios are not built for excitement. They are built for freedom.

The boring truth about wealth is that it is not a moment. It is a system.

And systems are not exciting to talk about. They are not fun at dinner parties. But they work. They scale. They endure.

If you want entertainment, the market will give it to you. But it will also take your time, your energy, and your potential returns if you are not careful.

If you want results, you must choose another path.

The path that values simplicity over stimulation.

The path that trades thrills for peace.

The path that looks boring today but feels extraordinary tomorrow.

So build your system. Automate your plan. Choose your assets with care. Stick to them with conviction. Trust the process through the ups and downs.

And let time do the heavy lifting.

Because while the rest of the world is chasing excitement, you will be doing something far more powerful.

You will be building wealth.

Quietly. Steadily. Unapologetically.

And when it finally shows up in your life, it will not feel boring at all.

It will feel like freedom.

07
YOUR FREEDOM NUMBER

STOP CHASING MILLIONS. START DESIGNING YOUR NUMBER.

MAIN POINTS

» **Define What Wealth Means to You**
More than money, it's control, peace, and choices

» **How to Calculate Your Freedom Number**
Simple math, life-changing clarity

» **Replace Income with Yield**
How QQQ and SMH contribute to fu**ture cash flow**

» **Build for Autonomy, Not Opulence**
The wealth mindset that scales without ego

» **When Enough Is Actually Enough**
Avoiding the trap of perpetual dissatisfaction

» **The "Why" Behind the Wealth**
Anchor your investing to purpose, not just profit

DEFINE WHAT WEALTH MEANS TO YOU

MORE THAN MONEY, IT'S CONTROL, PEACE, AND CHOICES

Wealth means different things to different people. But for most, the default definition comes from the outside. Headlines. Social feeds. Cultural myths. Somewhere along the way, wealth became synonymous with a number. Ten million. Fifty million. Nine figures. More. Always more.

But the truth is no number means anything without context. Without clarity. Without a vision for how that number changes your life.

Wealth is not the size of your portfolio. It is the shape of your freedom.

It is the ability to make decisions without financial fear. It is the power to say yes to what matters and no to what does not. It is waking up in control of your time, your energy, and your attention. It is no longer trading your best hours for someone else's goals. It is breathing easier because your future is no longer fragile.

Wealth is not about escape. It is about alignment.

And that alignment starts with asking the one question most people never pause to answer.

What does wealth mean to you.

Not to your neighbor. Not to your boss. Not to your peers. To you.

What would change in your life if you had enough. What would you stop doing. What would you finally allow yourself to start. How would you show up in your relationships. How would you spend your time. What kind of work would you pursue if money were no longer the reason you had to do it.

These are not soft questions. They are the most strategic ones you will ever answer.

Because once you know what wealth means to you, every financial decision becomes easier. You no longer chase every new trend. You stop comparing your numbers to someone else's life. You stop looking at your portfolio as a scoreboard and start seeing it as a tool.

Wealth stops being abstract. It becomes personal.

Maybe for you, wealth means working three days a week and coaching your kids on the other two. Maybe it means leaving the city and buying land. Maybe it means building a creative business that pays your bills and fills your soul. Maybe it means retiring early and spending the next thirty years doing meaningful volunteer work.

Whatever it is, it starts with defining it on your own terms.

Without that definition, the default kicks in. You chase status. You build for approval. You accumulate without direction. You follow other people's maps and wonder why you still feel lost.

Defining wealth is not about shrinking your dreams. It is about sharpening them.

And once you have clarity, you can start building toward it with purpose. You can reverse engineer the life you want and begin to ask better questions.

How much income would that life require. How much capital would I need to generate that income. What is my timeline. What is my gap. What is my strategy for closing it.

That is where the freedom number comes in. It is not just a financial calculation. It is a reflection of your values. Your priorities. Your ideal rhythm of life.

Some people may find that their freedom number is lower than expected. Others may realize it is higher. Either way, the point is not the number itself. The point is that now you are building toward something real.

You are not chasing wealth as a concept. You are creating a path toward a defined outcome. A life that feels right. A life that reflects your deepest sense of alignment.

And once you define it, you protect it.

You stop letting distractions pull you into complexity. You stop letting fear make your decisions. You stop letting the market determine your emotions.

You start investing with clarity. With confidence. With calm.

Because now your portfolio has a purpose. It is not just growing for the sake of growing. It is moving toward something meaningful. It is building the life you actually want.

So pause and ask yourself. What would wealth do for me that I cannot do today. What do I want more of. What do I want less of. What does enough actually look like.

The answers will not come all at once. But once they start, everything else starts to make sense.

And that is the beginning of real wealth.

Not just having more.

But knowing why.

REPLACE INCOME WITH YIELD

HOW QQQ AND SMH CONTRIBUTE TO FUTURE CASH FLOW

When people think about financial freedom, they often imagine quitting their job and never needing to work again. But what really creates that possibility is not the absence of work. It is the presence of income that comes from somewhere other than your labor.

That shift from earned income to investment yield is the true unlock.

It is not about stopping work. It is about stopping dependence. It is about reaching the point where your money continues working even when you do not. Where your days are no longer dictated by necessity, but shaped by choice. That is when the freedom number becomes more than an idea. It becomes a system that pays you to live the life you designed.

To make that system real, you need assets that generate yield. Assets that produce income without requiring constant attention. Assets that grow and return value over time.

This is where QQQ and SMH play a critical role.

Both funds contain companies that generate substantial cash flow. These companies reinvest profits into research, innovation, infrastructure, and market expansion. Some pay dividends. Others reinvest heavily to drive growth that translates into rising share prices. Either way, they contribute to your portfolio's ability to deliver yield, whether through direct payments or capital appreciation.

Let us unpack what that means for you.

Imagine you have reached your freedom number. You are no longer working for income. You are living off the returns your portfolio generates. That return may come in the form of dividends, which can be taken as cash. Or it may come from systematic withdrawals of appreciated capital. Either way, your lifestyle is supported by yield, not wages.

If your portfolio includes **QQQ**, you are drawing from companies like Apple, Microsoft, and Amazon. These are businesses with global scale, strong margins, and product ecosystems that continue to produce recurring revenue. Their performance is not built on hype. It is built on habits. People use their services daily. Enterprises run on their platforms. Nations rely on their infrastructure. That kind of relevance translates into durable returns.

SMH adds another dimension. It gives you exposure to semiconductor companies like **NVIDIA**, Taiwan Semiconductor, and Broadcom. These companies may be less visible to the average consumer, but they power everything from smartphones to data centers to electric vehicles. Their role in the global economy is not optional. It is foundational. As long as the world keeps digitizing, these firms keep growing. And that growth can become yield.

Some investors think yield only comes from bonds or high-dividend stocks. That is a narrow view. In a well-structured plan, yield includes any return that can be used to support your lifestyle. If your holdings appreciate and you withdraw a portion each year within a sustainable range, you are still harvesting yield, just in the form of controlled drawdowns rather than passive distributions.

And because QQQ and SMH are both composed of highly liquid and transparent assets, they allow you to access that yield with flexibility. You are not locked into fixed payouts or rigid terms. You have control. You have options. You have access.

This is how freedom is built.

By replacing dependence on a paycheck with a system that generates income in your sleep.

But that system does not build itself.

It requires consistency. It requires contribution. It requires alignment between your capital and the companies best positioned to generate long-term value.

That is why allocating to QQQ and SMH is not just about growth. It is about positioning. You are buying into the business models that define the modern economy. You are participating in the same sectors that drive productivity, power innovation, and deliver results for the world's most sophisticated investors.

And as your portfolio grows, you are not just building wealth. You are building income. Income that reflects the value your capital is helping to create.

This is the difference between trading and designing.

Traders chase movement. Builders design yield. Builders ask how they can transform capital into cash flow without sacrificing their time or peace of mind.

That is the strategy that scales.

Because once you learn how to replace your income with yield, everything changes.

You are no longer asking how much longer you need to work.

You are asking how much freedom you are already earning.

And that answer grows every year you stay committed to the system you are building.

BUILD FOR AUTONOMY, NOT OPULENCE

THE WEALTH MINDSET THAT SCALES WITHOUT EGO

There is a version of wealth that gets celebrated everywhere. The luxury cars. The massive homes. The private jets. The exclusive vacations. This is the story of wealth that sells magazines and drives clicks. It is dramatic. It is visible. It is loud.

But it is not the only version of wealth. And it is not always the most powerful.

For many, the most valuable form of wealth is not measured in possessions. It is measured in autonomy. The ability to decide how you spend your time. The ability to say no without consequence. The ability to walk away from noise and choose clarity. That is real power. And it rarely shows up on social media.

Building for autonomy means designing a life where your values guide your actions, not your obligations. It means owning your mornings. Protecting your attention. Prioritizing work that brings energy rather than just income. It means shifting the entire focus of your financial plan away from appearances and toward alignment.

That shift requires a different mindset. It requires letting go of the idea that wealth needs to be proven. That success needs to be performed. That freedom must look like extravagance. Because when you build for autonomy, you are not building to impress. You are building to live.

And that kind of wealth scales without ego.

You stop chasing lifestyle inflation. You stop needing to earn more just to spend more. You stop trying to upgrade your life for the approval of people who are not even watching.

Instead, you build a system that pays you in flexibility. You create margin in your life. You open space for creativity, for rest, for contribution. You make room for the parts of life that do not show up in spreadsheets but define how fulfilled you feel at the end of each day.

This is the mindset that actually sustains wealth. Because it keeps you grounded. It keeps you focused on what matters. It protects you from the spiral of more, for the sake of more.

If your definition of success requires constant external validation, you will always feel behind. There will always be someone with more. A better return. A bigger fund. A flashier asset. That comparison trap is endless. And it drains your energy.

But when your goal is autonomy, the game changes. Your portfolio is no longer about dominance. It is about direction. Every contribution you make is not for ego. It is for ownership. Ownership of your schedule. Ownership of your work. Ownership of your story.

That is why investing in scalable assets like SMH and QQQ is not about luxury. It is about leverage. These funds give you exposure to the most productive engines of the global economy. They allow you to participate in innovation without needing to manage every detail. They allow you to benefit from progress without sacrificing your attention to constant management.

This is how you scale your life.

You scale it by letting your capital work while you focus on what matters most.

That might be building a business. Raising a family. Mentoring others. Creating something meaningful. Supporting causes that reflect your values. Whatever it is, you are now resourced to lead it from a place of strength.

That strength does not come from opulence. It comes from clarity. Clarity around what you are building. Clarity around what enough looks like. Clarity around how you define a rich life on your own terms.

You do not need the world's approval to build that life. You need alignment.

Because when wealth becomes a tool for freedom, not for display, you win twice. You build without pressure. And you live without apology.

And in a world obsessed with what wealth looks like, there is something powerful about knowing exactly what it feels like.

It feels calm. It feels clear. It feels yours.

WHEN ENOUGH IS ACTUALLY ENOUGH

AVOIDING THE TRAP OF PERPETUAL DISSATISFACTION

There is a moment every serious investor must face. A moment that comes not at the beginning of the journey, but at the peak. When the numbers look strong. When the systems are working. When the plan is ahead of schedule. The moment is quiet, but the question is loud.

Is this enough.

And the challenge is that most people never answer it. They keep moving. They keep growing. They keep accumulating. Because that is what they have been trained to do. More is always better. Bigger portfolio. Higher yield. Faster compounding. The idea of stopping, or even slowing down, feels like quitting.

But at some point, you have to decide what you are actually building. A life or a ladder.

Ladders never end. They just keep going. Every new rung reveals another. Every milestone resets expectations. And without a clear sense of what enough looks like, the climb becomes automatic. Reflexive. Even exhausting.

This is how people become wealthy and stay anxious. They never define the finish line. They never allow themselves to arrive.

Enough is not about limitation. It is about liberation. It is the recognition that the goal was never infinite accumulation. The goal was to build a life you could fully own. A life that reflects your values. A life with space to breathe. Enough means you can stop chasing and start choosing.

But to declare enough, you need courage. You need to step off the track that everyone else is still running. You need to stop measuring yourself by comparison and start measuring yourself by alignment. You need to replace ambition for its own sake with ambition in service of a larger purpose

Enough is different for everyone. For some, it means a paid-off home and a modest portfolio that covers living expenses. For others, it means building intergenerational wealth. For others still, it means creating time to work on projects that may never pay but always fulfill.

The number matters less than the awareness. You must know what you are solving for. You must know the life you are trying to fund. And when the math shows you that you are already there, or close to it, you must be willing to shift your mindset.

Not from growth to stagnation. But from growth to stewardship.

That shift is subtle but profound.

When you are chasing, every gain fuels urgency. When you are living from enough, every gain fuels peace. When you are chasing, the market feels like a scoreboard. When you are living from enough, the market becomes a tool. When you are chasing, time feels scarce. When you are living from enough, time feels abundant.

This does not mean you stop investing. It means you stop waiting to feel secure. You stop telling yourself that one more zero will change everything. You stop believing that joy is always just around the corner of the next milestone.

Enough allows you to be fully present in the life you already built.

And it gives you the clarity to say no. No to noise. No to deals that distract. No to pressure that pulls you away from what matters. Because enough is not just a number in your account. It is a posture. It is a mindset that says you trust your plan. You trust your process. And you no longer need to prove anything.

This is where your freedom number finds its full power. Not just as a financial threshold. But as a psychological release. When you know your number, and you see that you have reached it, or that your trajectory will take you there, you gain permission to shift your posture.

You can focus on health. Relationships. Contribution. Craft. Community. You can reinvest your energy into areas of life that compound in ways spreadsheets will never show.

And that kind of wealth is the rarest of all. Because it is not loud. It is not flashy. But it is deeply fulfilling.

You know you have enough when you no longer ask what the market can give you. You start asking what your life can give others. What your time can unlock. What your presence can make possible.

Because when you define enough, you unlock everything that more was supposed to deliver.

And you get to live from that place every day.

THE WHY BEHIND THE WEALTH

ANCHOR YOUR INVESTING TO PURPOSE, NOT JUST PROFIT

At some point in the journey, the spreadsheets are done. The numbers are clear. The strategy is working. You know what to invest. You know how much to contribute. You understand your risk tolerance. You have run the simulations. You have calculated your freedom number. The structure is solid.

But the structure alone is not enough.

Because a system without a soul cannot sustain you. A plan without a purpose cannot fulfill you. If you do not connect your investing to a deeper why, then wealth becomes a loop instead of a launchpad. You end up optimizing without direction. Winning without meaning.

The why is what makes the numbers matter.

The why is what turns discipline into devotion. It is what allows you to stick with your plan through uncertainty. It is what helps you resist temptation, ignore noise, and stay grounded when the market pulls at your emotions. It is the answer to the question no spreadsheet can answer: What is all of this really for?

Maybe your why is family. You want to spend more time with your children. You want to be present for milestones. You want to create opportunities for them that you never had. Maybe your why is freedom. You want to wake up without an alarm clock. You want to work on projects that excite you. You want to live life without constantly thinking about bills and budgets.

Maybe your why is contribution. You want to fund causes that matter. You want to give generously without fear. You want to use your time and resources to move the world forward in ways that reflect your values.

Or maybe your why is simply peace. You want to slow down. To rest. To enjoy your days without the constant hum of financial anxiety in the background.

There is no right why. There is only your why.

And once you are clear on it, everything else gets easier.

You start to invest with intention. You stop chasing returns just to see bigger numbers on a screen. You start thinking about what those numbers will actually allow you to do. You start seeing every contribution as a brick in the foundation of your future life. You start protecting your plan not out of fear, but out of love for what it makes possible.

The best investors in the world are not just disciplined. They are anchored. They know exactly why they are building what they are building. That clarity gives them strength. It makes them less reactive and more resolved. They do not let market headlines shake them. They do not need constant excitement to stay engaged. They are not addicted to the thrill of speculation. They are grounded in something much deeper.

And that grounding is available to anyone who chooses to define it.

It does not require a massive net worth. It requires honest reflection. It requires asking what success really means to you. It requires separating your goals from someone else's expectations. It requires the courage to build a portfolio that reflects your purpose, not your ego.

Because wealth without purpose becomes pressure. But wealth with purpose becomes power.

The power to live on your terms. The power to show up fully for the people you care about. The power to shape your days instead of reacting to them. The power to look back and know that you did not just accumulate, you created something meaningful.

And that is why this chapter matters so much.

Your freedom number is not just a calculation. It is a calling. It is the invitation to stop chasing someone else's version of success and start designing your own. It is the moment you take control of your future, not just with numbers, but with narrative. It is the moment you begin to lead, not just your investments, but your life.

So ask yourself now, and ask yourself often. What is my why. What am I really building. Who am I building it for. What kind of life do I want to wake up into. What do I want to give. What do I want to remember. What do I want to feel when I arrive.

Answer those questions and your portfolio will become more than a financial tool.

It will become a mirror of your purpose.

And that is when wealth begins to work in its highest form.

Not as a number. Not as a goal.

But as a life that feels fully yours.

08
THE 3 ENEMIES OF WEALTH

WHAT SILENTLY ERODES YOUR FUTURE,
AND HOW TO FIGHT BACK

MAIN POINTS

» **Inflation: The Invisible Thief**
Why cash alone won't cut it

» **Lifestyle Creep**
How upgraded habits destroy upgraded incomes

» **Procrastination: The Costliest Decision**
What waiting even one year can cost you

» **Taxes and Fees: The Quiet Drains**
How to optimize without obsessing

» **The Myth of Someday**
Why there's no perfect moment to start

» **Your Environment Shapes Your Net Worth**
Align your circle with your financial future

INFLATION THE INVISIBLE THIEF

WHY CASH ALONE WILL NOT CUT IT

Most people think the greatest risk to their financial future is losing money. A bad investment. A market downturn. A failed business. But the truth is often more subtle and far more dangerous.

The greatest threat to wealth is not a dramatic collapse. It is slow erosion.

And inflation is the most relentless force behind it.

Inflation does not steal in the open. It does not trigger fear the way a market crash might. It does not make headlines unless it spikes. But it is always there. Quiet. Constant. Unforgiving. Every year, it chips away at the purchasing power of your money. Not all at once, but year after year after year.

And that is what makes it so dangerous. It feels like nothing is happening. Your account balance is stable. Your savings look untouched. But behind the scenes, everything you depend on- housing, food, healthcare, education, and travel- is becoming more expensive. And your money is quietly losing its ability to buy the life you want.

This is why holding too much cash is not a strategy. It is a slow decline.

There is a place for emergency funds. There is value in liquidity. But beyond that, cash is not safety. It is exposure. If inflation averages two percent and your money earns zero point five percent in a savings account, you are losing one and a half percent every year. If inflation jumps to four or five percent as it has in recent cycles, your losses accelerate. You are standing still on paper, but moving backward in reality.

Over a decade, that gap compounds. What you thought was a cushion becomes a trap. You saved diligently. You were conservative. You avoided risk. And yet you arrive ten or twenty years later with less real value than when you started.

That is the invisible theft of inflation.

It punishes inaction. It penalizes hesitation. And it silently widens the gap between what you have and what you need.

This is why investing is not optional. It is essential.

It is not about chasing returns or becoming a market expert. It is about protecting the value of your time and your labor. It is about keeping pace with the rising cost of everything around you. It is about placing your capital into assets that do not shrink in value over time but grow alongside the world.

And that is where funds like QQQ and SMH become more than just opportunities. They become shields.

They give you exposure to companies that are not just surviving inflation but driving the solutions to it. Companies with pricing power. Companies with global scale. Companies that sit at the intersection of technology, productivity, and necessity. These are not guesses. They are positions in the future economy. And the future economy is where inflation gets absorbed, challenged, and in some cases, outpaced.

When you invest in innovation, you do more than grow your money. You defend it.

You give yourself a path to not just stay even, but get ahead. You give your future the tools to remain flexible. You stop letting inflation dictate your options. You stop watching your savings lose value while you wait for the perfect moment to start.

And you begin to play offense.

Because inflation will not wait for you to feel ready. It will not pause for better timing. It will not slow down out of fairness. It will do what it has always done. Take value away from those who are not actively protecting it.

The good news is that the solution is within reach. You do not need complexity. You need clarity. You need conviction. You need to move your money from idle to active. From losing ground to gaining ground.

That does not mean being reckless. It means being real.

Inflation is real. Its impact is real. And your response must be real too.

So when someone says they are waiting because they do not want to lose money, remember this.

If you are holding cash and doing nothing, you already are.

And the longer you wait, the less you will have to wait with.

HOW UPGRADED HABITS DESTROY UPGRADED INCOMES

The moment you start earning more, the world starts pulling at you. It is subtle at first. A better phone. A newer car. A bigger place. A nicer vacation. You tell yourself it is a reward. You worked hard. You deserve it. And maybe you do.

But over time, something dangerous begins to happen. Your spending grows faster than your investing. Your standard of living expands faster than your wealth. And without realizing it, you have stepped into a trap that captures millions of high earners.

Lifestyle creep.

This is one of the most silent and consistent destroyers of long-term wealth. It does not announce itself. It does not feel reckless. It feels normal. It feels deserved. It feels like progress. But behind that illusion, it is consuming the very financial margin you need to create real freedom.

You make more. You spend more. You invest the same. Or less.

That equation might not hurt in your twenties. Or even in your thirties. But over decades, the compounding impact is massive. The person who increases their lifestyle every time their income increases never builds a true buffer. They never break free of the need to earn. They are locked into a higher burn rate and often a higher level of stress.

It does not matter if your income triples. If your expenses triple too, you are in the same place with a nicer wardrobe and more expensive problems.

Lifestyle creep is dangerous because it hides inside what looks like success. You got the raise. You closed the deal. You upgraded your home. You posted the vacation. On the outside, everything signals forward motion. But internally, the system is fragile. The margin is gone. The flexibility is gone. You are working harder than ever, but you are not free.

That is the great lie of lifestyle inflation. It offers comfort today and steals freedom tomorrow.

This is not a call to live small. It is a call to live aligned.

There is nothing wrong with enjoying your success. But enjoyment and excess are not the same. You can travel without overcommitting. You can buy quality without overextending. You can live beautifully and still build wealth if your investments grow faster than your lifestyle.

The key is deciding early what enough looks like. Not as a limit. As a design.

Design a life that feels rich now and gets richer later. Design a system where every increase in income feeds your future first. Before the car. Before the vacation. Before the restaurant upgrade. Funnel a portion of every raise directly into your investment engine. Let that engine scale while your life stays grounded.

That is where real peace comes from. Not from earning more. From needing less.

And ironically, when your lifestyle stays stable and your wealth grows, you gain the very thing lifestyle creep promises but never delivers: Freedom.

Freedom to stop when you want. Freedom to say no. Freedom to change direction. Freedom to invest in people and projects without asking for permission or calculating the cost.

Wealth is not what you earn. It is what you keep. It is what you own. It is what keeps growing when your income stops.

And the enemy of that kind of wealth is not bad luck. It is unchecked comfort. Upgraded defaults. Automatic yeses that become permanent costs.

So pause before every lifestyle decision and ask a better question.

Is this aligned with the life I want to build. Or is this just a reflection of the life others expect me to live.

Because lifestyle creep does not show up all at once. It shows up one small decision at a time.

And each time you say yes to an upgrade, you are saying no to something else. You are trading a little bit of freedom for a little bit of comfort.

The question is whether that trade is worth it.

And whether it still will be ten years from now.

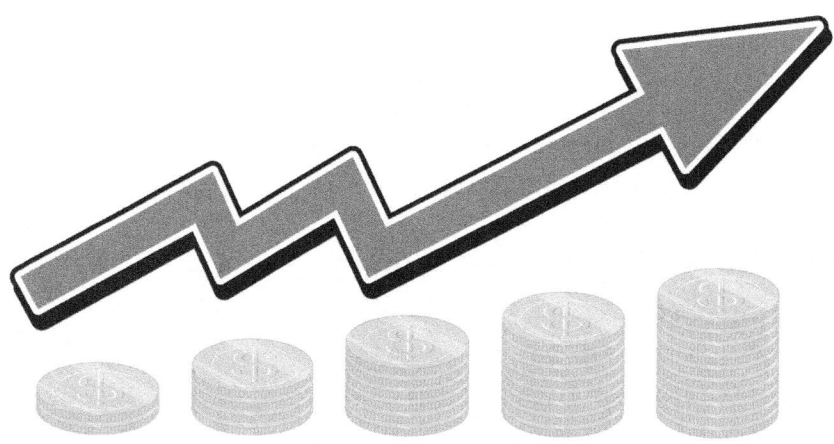

PROCRASTINATION THE COSTLIEST DECISION

WHAT WAITING EVEN ONE YEAR CAN COST YOU

We all tell ourselves the same lie at some point.

I will start soon.

When I get the raise. When I pay off the loan. When the market settles. When things slow down. When I feel more confident. When the timing is better. There is always a reason to wait. And on the surface, each reason sounds reasonable. Responsible. Even strategic.

But beneath that surface is a truth that does not care about our excuses.

Every year you wait, you pay.

Not in stress. Not in guilt. In dollars. Real, irreversible dollars. Dollars you can never get back. Dollars that would have compounded for you if they had been given the time. Dollars that were lost not from risk or volatility, but from indecision.

Procrastination is not just a delay. It is a cost. A compounding cost.

Because the most powerful lever in wealth building is time. More than return. More than income. More than any single decision. Time multiplies everything. And once it is gone, it does not come back.

Start investing at twenty-five instead of thirty-five and the difference can be hundreds of thousands of dollars. Not because you contributed more. Because you started earlier. Start at thirty-five instead of forty-five and the same pattern repeats. Wealth does not reward the smartest investor. It rewards the earliest committed investor.

Every year you delay is a year your money does not get to work. A year you miss out on compounding. A year you stay exposed to inflation. A year your freedom stays on hold. That is the cost. And it does not show up on your statement. It shows up in what you never get to experience.

Fewer choices. Less margin. More pressure to catch up.

And catching up is always more expensive than starting on time.

Because once you fall behind, you have to contribute more. Take on more risk. Rely more on perfect timing. And the more you rely on perfection, the more fragile your plan becomes.

This is why the market does not reward hesitation. It rewards participation.

You do not need to have it all figured out. You do not need to invest a fortune. You need to start. You need to build the habit. You need to get your capital into the system where it can begin to do what it was meant to do.

Work for you.

The beauty of ETFs like QQQ and SMH is that they make this process simple. You do not need to pick individual stocks. You do not need to study technicals. You do not need to guess. You allocate to vehicles that give you broad exposure to the most productive sectors of the economy. You buy into innovation. You hold positions that grow with global demand. And you let time magnify your decision.

That decision only needs to happen once.

Once you commit, the system can take over. Contributions can be automated. Growth can be reinvested. Your attention can return to life while your capital keeps building.

But it starts with now. Not next week. Not next year. Not after the next election or the next market cycle.

Because someday is not a plan. Someday is a placeholder.

The only time that compounds is the time you actually use.

And every month you wait is a month your future pays for.

So if you are wondering when to start, the answer is not a date on a calendar.

The answer is the moment you stop asking and start moving.

Because wealth is not built by waiting.

It is built by beginning.

TAXES AND FEES THE QUIET DRAINS
HOW TO OPTIMIZE WITHOUT OBSESSING

There are two forces that quietly siphon wealth from even the smartest investors. You do not always see them. They do not make headlines. They do not trigger panic. But they are there. Steady. Unemotional. Relentless. Every year. Every quarter. Every transaction. And if you do not pay attention to them, they can undo years of effort.

Taxes and fees.

Not the kind that shows up in big moments. The kind that accumulates in the background. Hidden in statements. Baked into fine print. Accepted as normal.

But normal does not mean harmless.

Start with fees. They may look small. A one percent management fee. A small advisory charge. An account maintenance line item. But over a long investing horizon, even a small percentage compounds into a large cost. If your portfolio grows to one million dollars, one percent is ten thousand dollars every single year. That money is not growing for you. It is growing for someone else.

Now imagine that over ten or twenty years. That is not a fee. That is a transfer of wealth.

And it is often completely avoidable.

Low fee investment options exist for a reason. Funds like QQQ and SMH are powerful not just because of their performance, but because of their structure. They offer broad exposure to innovative, high quality companies with extremely low internal costs. They do not require active management. They do not generate endless advisory bills. They do what most expensive funds fail to do: Deliver long term returns at scale, efficiently.

You should never pay for complexity when simplicity delivers better results.

Now look at taxes. Here, the issue is not just how much you pay, but how often. Every time you sell an asset for a gain, you create a tax event. And the more frequently you trade, the more taxable events you create. Short term capital gains are taxed at higher rates. That means every flip, every rotation, every reaction to market noise could be silently reducing your net return.

This is why long term holding is not just a strategy for growth. It is a strategy for tax efficiency.

Hold quality assets for the long run, and you defer taxes until you actually need the money. Invest through tax advantaged accounts, and you may eliminate or reduce that liability entirely. Use tax loss harvesting intelligently, and you can offset gains with losses when appropriate. None of these strategies require you to become an expert. They simply require awareness.

Because the truth is this. No one will protect your net return except you.

The system is not designed for optimization. It is designed for friction. And friction always benefits the institutions more than the investor.

But the good news is that you do not need to obsess. You just need to pay attention to the basics.

Choose low fee funds. Avoid unnecessary trading. Use accounts that match your long term goals. Reinvest gains instead of trying to time exits. And ask better questions before every move.

What is the real cost of this decision. Not just the potential return. The actual impact on my portfolio after fees and taxes.

Wealth is not just about growth. It is about retention. It is about keeping more of what you earn. Protecting more of what you build. Defending more of what you are giving your time and energy to create.

Because if you are not paying attention to these quiet drains, they will keep working against you while your strategy is working for you.

And over time, the result will not just be smaller gains.

It will be a future that was more expensive than it needed to be.

THE MYTH OF SOMEDAY

WHY THERE IS NO PERFECT MOMENT TO START

Someday feels safe.

It gives you space. It gives you an excuse. It sounds responsible. It sounds thoughtful. It sounds like patience. But someday is often not a strategy. It is a delay. It is the polite name we give to fear. It is the story we tell ourselves to avoid the discomfort of beginning.

I will start investing when I have more time. When I understand more. When I feel more confident. When the market is calmer. When the economy looks better. When I clear my debt. When I get the new job. When the bonus hits.

When.

Always when.

But the market does not wait. Compounding does not pause. Inflation does not take a break. Opportunity does not check your calendar before moving forward.

And while you wait for the perfect conditions, time quietly does its work.

The missed returns. The lost contributions. The delayed growth. These do not show up as dramatic events. They show up as absence. The absence of momentum. The absence of options. The absence of progress.

The most powerful force in wealth creation is not return. It is time in the market. And time only works for you if you put your money to work. Otherwise, it becomes a cost. A silent erosion of potential.

The perfect moment is not coming.

Because every moment comes with a new uncertainty. Rates go up. Markets drop. Elections approach. Recessions get predicted. And through all of it, the market continues its long upward march. Not in a straight line. Not without pain. But with resilience.

Ask anyone who started ten years ago whether they wish they had waited for a better time. They do not. Because what looked like a turbulent starting point became the beginning of a long and powerful wealth journey.

The danger is not in bad timing. The danger is in no timing at all.

Starting imperfectly will always beat waiting forever. A modest portfolio in motion is more powerful than a large one that lives in theory. You can refine your strategy as you go. You can learn while invested. You can adjust once you are moving. But you cannot compound what you never begin.

This is why the myth of someday is so dangerous. It keeps you feeling safe while you fall behind. It keeps you feeling prudent while you miss the entire point. Wealth does not require precision. It requires participation.

And participation begins with one step.

A small contribution. An automatic transfer. A single decision to begin owning the future instead of waiting for permission to engage it.

You do not need to understand everything. You do not need to optimize everything. You need to move. Because motion beats hesitation. Always.

You can start small. You can start slowly. But the only unacceptable path is to keep waiting for perfect.

Perfect does not exist.

There is only now. And the longer you wait to claim it, the more expensive the wait becomes.

So the question is not whether now is ideal.

The question is whether someday is even real.

Because the people who build wealth are not the ones who start perfectly.

They are the ones who stop waiting.

YOUR ENVIRONMENT SHAPES YOUR NET WORTH

ALIGN YOUR CIRCLE WITH YOUR FINANCIAL FUTURE

Most conversations about money focus on what to do. What to invest in. How much to save. Where to allocate. How to reduce risk. These are important questions. But they all assume one thing, that your decision-making is your own.

It is not.

Your beliefs about money, your behaviors around risk, your sense of what is possible or necessary, none of these exist in a vacuum. They are shaped by the people you listen to. The people you spend time with. The stories you hear every day. The questions you are asked. The standards you are surrounded by.

Environment is not neutral. It pulls you in a direction.

Sit with people who treat money like a game and you will be tempted to gamble. Sit with people who fear every fluctuation and you will struggle to stay invested. Sit with people who treat wealth as shameful and you may sabotage your own progress just to stay accepted.

Now sit with people who are building. People who are thoughtful about what they own. People who talk about time horizons instead of headlines. People who make investing feel normal, not risky. That circle will not just change your financial strategy. It will raise your standard for what is possible.

Because what you believe is often a reflection of what the people around you believe. What you normalize becomes what you expect. If everyone you know is chasing trends or living beyond their means or putting off the hard conversations, you will find yourself doing the same. Not because you decided to. Because you stopped noticing it.

This is the hidden danger. Environment does not shout. It whispers. It turns bad advice into background noise. It turns distraction into default. And the longer you stay in the wrong room, the harder it becomes to see the difference between what feels normal and what is actually useful.

So audit your circle.

Who do you talk to about money. Are they moving toward financial independence or just spending more every time they earn more. Do they ask better questions or repeat old fears. Do they share strategies or simply vent about stress. Do they encourage you to grow or help you justify staying the same.

You do not need a room full of experts. You need a room full of people who are moving in the same direction.

People who value ownership. People who play the long game. People who understand that money is not just about accumulation. It is about alignment. It is about building a life you control. A life you can hand to your children with pride. A life where your decisions are not shaped by fear or urgency or scarcity.

And if your current environment does not support that, build a new one.

Read different books. Follow different voices. Join different conversations. Find mentors who reflect your future, not just your present. Listen to people who have already walked the path. Spend time with those who do not flinch at discipline, who do not apologize for ambition, and who do not compromise on the things that matter most.

Your net worth is not just about money. It is about mindset. And mindset is contagious.

If you are serious about changing your financial future, change the room you are in.

Because the right environment will not just support your plan.

It will strengthen it.

MAIN POINTS

» **Start Small, Think Big, Move Fast**
Action beats perfection

» **Repetition Builds Wealth, Not Genius**
Why doing the boring work wins big

» **Your Life is the Portfolio That Matters**
Build wealth to serve your goals, not just grow numbers

» **The Legacy of Intentional Investing**
What you pass on is more than money

» **You Don't Need Permission**
The freedom to build, the courage to hold

» **From Investor to Architect**
Design a future where you own your time, your choices, and your impact

START SMALL THINK BIG MOVE FAST

ACTION BEATS PERFECTION

Most people never build wealth because they wait too long for a perfect plan. They want every detail to be locked in. They want absolute certainty. They want to feel ready. But in the pursuit of perfect, they never begin. They stay stuck in research. They stay stuck in analysis. They stay stuck in fear disguised as preparation.

Meanwhile, time keeps moving. Markets keep growing. Opportunities keep compounding. And the people who win are not the ones with the most sophisticated strategy. They are the ones who started. They are the ones who built momentum when others waited for clarity.

Start small. Think big. Move fast.

That is the formula. Not because it is trendy. Because it works.

Start small means you do not wait for a massive windfall or a perfect income. You begin with what you have. One hundred dollars. Five hundred. A percentage of every paycheck. You automate it. You remove friction. You treat your investment like a non-negotiable. You commit to movement, not magnitude.

Think big means you connect your small action to a long term vision. You see your contribution not just as a number but as the first step in a life where work becomes optional. Where decisions are made from strength, not survival. Where your days reflect your values and not just your obligations. You think in decades. You zoom out. You anchor every short term action to the freedom you are building for your future self.

Move fast means you do not overthink the basics. You choose simple assets that reflect the economy you believe in. You allocate to scalable engines of innovation. You take ownership of your timeline. You stop waiting for reassurance from people who are not building what you are building. You stop asking for a guarantee and start trusting your process.

The wealthiest people in the world are not the smartest. They are not the most accurate. They are the most consistent. They understood earlier than most that motion creates insight. That action creates data. That investing is not about perfect timing but about time itself.

Every day you wait costs more than the day before. Not just in money. In opportunity. In peace of mind. In optionality. The sooner you start, the sooner your money starts working alongside you. And the sooner you get to stop doing all the work yourself.

This is the mindset that separates those who talk about wealth from those who live it.

Start with a recurring investment into QQQ or SMH. Choose one. Automate it. Let it run. Watch it grow. Then increase it. Scale it with your income. Add to it with every raise. Every bonus. Every unexpected gain. Turn the habit into a system. Then turn the system into a legacy.

Do not wait for confidence to show up. Confidence is not what creates action. Action is what creates confidence. You begin scared. You begin unsure. But you begin anyway.

And then one day you look back and realize you did not just build a portfolio.

You built the capacity to act.

You built the muscle of ownership.

You built a life that no longer depends on someone else's approval.

That is what happens when you start small and move fast.

You stop hoping for change and start creating it.

So if you are on the edge of starting, this is your moment.

Not next quarter. Not after the next market dip. Not once you finish one more book or watch one more video.

Now.

Because everything you want on the other side of freedom is waiting for one decision.

To begin.

REPETITION BUILDS WEALTH NOT GENIUS
WHY DOING THE BORING WORK WINS BIG

We live in a world obsessed with genius. People chase hacks. They glorify bold predictions. They search for the next big thing. The assumption is that success comes from knowing something no one else knows. From being early. From being clever. But wealth rarely works that way.

The truth is simple. The people who build extraordinary wealth are not the most brilliant. They are the most consistent. They find what works and they do it over and over again.

Repetition is not boring. It is strategic.

It is how habits become systems. It is how momentum becomes inevitability. It is how small daily actions compound into life-changing outcomes. And the reason most people never experience this is because they abandon what works too early. They get bored. They chase novelty. They confuse motion with progress.

But the market does not reward motion. It rewards endurance.

The investor who contributes the same amount every month for twenty years will almost always outperform the investor who jumps in and out based on fear, emotion, or prediction. The key is not finding the perfect moment. The key is never breaking the chain.

This is why automated investing is so powerful. It removes the friction of decision. It removes the temptation to tweak. It keeps your strategy boring, which is exactly what allows your results to become exciting.

You do not need to time the market. You need to show up for it.

Buy QQQ every month. Add SMH when you can. Reinvest the dividends. Resist the urge to optimize. Ignore the noise. Let time do its job. That is the work. It will never go viral. It will never sound like a secret. But it is the most proven path to financial freedom ever created.

And here is the irony. Repetition does not mean you are stuck. It means you are scaling.

Every cycle adds experience. Every contribution adds capital. Every lesson adds conviction. Over time, what felt like a simple plan becomes a force. It becomes your financial engine. It becomes the quiet power behind every bold decision you make in life.

Want to change careers. Want to travel more. Want to take a break. Want to help your kids. Want to fund a mission. Want to walk away. All of those choices become available when your system is running without you.

And that system only works if you keep showing up.

The work that builds wealth is not the same as the work that builds attention. You do not need genius. You need grit. You need discipline. You need to love the part that most people overlook. The calendar reminder. The monthly transfer. The simple buy. The boring check-in.

Because here is the truth no one talks about. Wealth is often invisible while it is growing. It does not feel like progress. It feels like routine. But then one day it tips. And when it does, it changes everything.

You do not need to be brilliant. You need to be repeatable.

You do not need to be first. You need to be faithful to your plan.

You do not need to impress anyone. You need to keep going when no one is watching.

Repetition is what makes compounding possible.

So do not chase excitement.

Chase execution.

Because every time you repeat the right behavior, you are not just investing money.

You are reinforcing identity.

You are becoming someone who builds. Someone who finishes. Someone who earns freedom the way it is always earned.

Quietly. Consistently. Relentlessly.

YOUR LIFE IS THE PORTFOLIO THAT MATTERS

BUILD WEALTH TO SERVE YOUR GOALS NOT JUST GROW NUMBERS

Numbers are easy to track. They go up or down. They fit into charts. They give you something to measure. That is why most people obsess over them. Portfolio value. Net worth. Asset allocation. But numbers are only part of the story. If you build a portfolio that performs and a life that does not, you missed the point.

Wealth is not the goal. Wealth is the tool.

The goal is how you live.

That means how you spend your time. Who you spend it with. What you create. What you contribute. What you protect. What you build when you are no longer burdened by financial anxiety. That is the real return. Not percentage points. Not headline performance. But the quality and clarity of your everyday life.

And that kind of return begins with alignment.

Your investing should reflect your values. Your portfolio should support your priorities. Your strategy should create space for the things that actually matter. If your money grows but your freedom shrinks, you are scaling in the wrong direction. If your wealth expands but your relationships contract, you are chasing the wrong goal.

This is not a call to retreat. It is a call to design.

You have an opportunity to treat your life like the portfolio that it is. Every decision is an allocation. Every habit is a position. Every hour is capital. Every conversation is either adding energy or extracting it. The same principles that build strong portfolios build strong lives.

Diversify where it counts. Concentrate where it matters. Rebalance when needed. Hold what grows. Cut what drags. Trust the long view. And measure your success not just by what you own, but by how you live.

This is why simplicity matters so much. When your financial strategy is clear and sustainable, your energy is freed up. You stop managing complexity and start managing intention. You stop checking your portfolio every day and start checking in with your purpose. You stop being reactive and start being present.

Owning SMH and QQQ is not just about exposure to growth. It is about giving your money a job. A job that funds your future. A job that gives you the ability to say yes when it matters and no when it counts. A job that supports your life instead of becoming your life.

You are not here to build wealth for the sake of wealth.

You are here to build the conditions for a life that reflects your deepest values.

That life may be quiet. Or adventurous. Or full of creation. Or dedicated to service. But whatever form it takes, it deserves to be built on purpose. And that purpose must show up in your strategy. Because without it, your portfolio becomes a disconnected engine. Always moving. Never arriving.

Money cannot tell you who you are. But it can fund the version of you that already knows.

So ask yourself the questions that do not show up in spreadsheets.

What do I want more of. What do I want less of. What am I building toward. What would a successful year feel like, not just financially, but emotionally, relationally, spiritually.

When you answer those questions, everything sharpens. You begin to see your wealth as fuel. Not identity. Not scoreboard. Not a substitute for purpose. Just fuel.

And that fuel allows you to go where you are meant to go.

Your life is the real portfolio. Everything else is structure.

So build your structure well. Make it efficient. Make it sustainable. Make it smart.

But never forget what it is supporting.

A life that is truly yours.

THE LEGACY OF INTENTIONAL INVESTING

WHAT YOU PASS ON IS MORE THAN MONEY

When most people hear the word legacy, they think of what gets left behind. An estate. A trust. A name etched on something permanent. But real legacy is not what happens after you are gone. Real legacy is the way your choices echo while you are still here. It is the example you set. The discipline you live. The story your children will tell about how you built and why you built it.

And legacy is built in the details.

It is built in the moments you said no to short term pleasure so you could say yes to long term peace. It is built in the decision to invest even when it felt uncomfortable. It is built in the quiet automation of wealth while the rest of the world chased noise. Legacy is not a moment. It is a pattern. A message repeated until it becomes part of who you are.

When you invest with intention, you send a message.

You show that money is not the point. Direction is. You show that wealth is not something you chase but something you align with. You show that freedom does not come from a number. It comes from clarity. That message is more powerful than any payout. It is the mindset that creates independence. And that mindset is what lasts.

Because what you pass on is not just assets. You pass on frameworks. Beliefs. Habits. You pass on how you responded to uncertainty. How you prioritized. How you made decisions when no one was watching. And those decisions become part of your family's financial vocabulary. They become stories. And stories become standards.

The people who leave the strongest legacy are not always the ones who made the most. They are the ones who made what they had count. They taught consistency. They modeled resilience. They spoke with confidence about the future because they were building it one contribution at a time.

That is what intentional investing creates.

It creates a track record that your children can study. It creates a map that others can follow. It removes the mystery around wealth and replaces it with clarity. You are no longer guessing. You are leading.

And leadership is the most powerful legacy of all.

You do not need a complex estate plan to begin this process. You need alignment. You need to know why you are investing and who you are investing for. You need to name your values. You need to speak them aloud. You need to bring others into the conversation early and often.

Talk to your children about what you own. Explain why you invest in QQQ. Explain what SMH represents. Help them see that wealth is not reserved for others. It is available to anyone who is willing to start. Help them understand that risk is not the enemy. Waste is. Show them how to take control instead of waiting for permission.

You are not just building for retirement. You are building for ripple effect.

A disciplined investor in one generation can change the entire trajectory of a family. Not because they passed on money. Because they passed on belief. Belief in ownership. Belief in structure. Belief in growth that is earned and then sustained.

That is what makes intentional investing so powerful. It is not emotional. It is educational. It teaches through action. It compounds far beyond the market. It shapes identity. It shifts what your family believes is possible.

And that shift is what transforms a portfolio into a legacy.

You do not need to be rich to start this process. You need to be intentional. You need to stop treating wealth as something separate from life. It is not separate. It is what funds the life that reflects your values.

So lead with clarity. Build with conviction. And share what you are building as you build it.

Because what you pass on is not just what you leave behind.

It is how you live right now.

YOU DO NOT NEED PERMISSION

THE FREEDOM TO BUILD
THE COURAGE TO HOLD

Most people are waiting for something.

Waiting for the perfect moment. Waiting for a sign. Waiting for someone to say they are ready. Waiting for confirmation that their plan is smart. Waiting for the market to calm down. Waiting for an expert to tell them they have what it takes.

But what they are really waiting for is permission.

Permission to begin. Permission to act. Permission to own the outcome. Permission to believe they are capable.

And that wait costs more than any mistake ever could.

No one is coming to give you permission. Not your manager. Not your financial advisor. Not the market. Not your parents. Not your friends. Everyone is too busy trying to figure out their own life. That is the truth no one says out loud. You have to choose yourself.

You do not need credentials to start investing. You do not need to read ten more books before you take action. You do not need to convince others that your approach makes sense. You do not need the world to understand your timeline, your priorities, or your reasons. You need one thing.

Conviction.

Conviction that your future deserves to be owned. That your freedom does not need validation. That your choices are not on trial. That clarity is more important than consensus.

The world will always offer reasons to wait. There will always be someone smarter. Someone louder. Someone more confident. But none of them will live your life. None of them will pay your bills. None of them will walk in your shoes when the time comes to pivot, to rest, to give, or to retire.

So stop explaining your plan. Start building it.

If you believe in technology, own it. If you believe in global innovation, invest in it. If you believe in semiconductors as the infrastructure of the future, add SMH to your portfolio. If you believe that scalable digital platforms will define the next generation of growth, let QQQ do its work.

You are not betting. You are positioning.

You are not hoping. You are allocating.

You are not waiting. You are deciding.

That shift, from seeking permission to taking ownership, is the moment everything begins to change. You stop outsourcing confidence. You stop needing constant affirmation. You stop feeling behind.

Because ownership is not just a financial act. It is an identity shift.

You become the person who acts. The person who creates space for change. The person who has their own strategy instead of borrowing someone else's opinion. The person who stays calm when others panic. The person who leads quietly through clarity.

That is who you are becoming every time you contribute. Every time you stay in. Every time you ignore the noise and return to the plan.

You are not just building a portfolio. You are becoming someone who no longer needs permission to build anything.

Your career. Your peace. Your relationships. Your freedom.

That permission has always been yours.

Now it is time to use it.

FROM INVESTOR TO ARCHITECT

DESIGN A FUTURE WHERE YOU OWN YOUR TIME YOUR CHOICES AND YOUR IMPACT

You started as an investor. You took the first step. You opened the account. You made your contribution. You stayed the course. But somewhere along the way, something more powerful happened. You became the architect.

Investing is not just about growing money. It is about designing a life. And when you step into that role fully, you begin to realize that you are not just reacting to opportunity. You are creating it. You are not just managing money. You are shaping your future.

That shift is what separates those who dabble from those who build.

Architects do not wait for conditions to be perfect. They work with what they have. They think structurally. They think about the long term. They connect every small detail to a larger vision. They do not just accumulate. They align. They design systems that serve goals, not systems that demand attention.

You now have that same ability.

Your portfolio is not a side project. It is part of the architecture of your life. Each investment is a building block. Each contribution is a beam. Each reinvested dividend is another layer of strength. Over time, those layers become structure. And that structure begins to support something greater than financial gain.

It supports freedom of time. The ability to work when you choose, not when you must.

It supports clarity of choice. The power to walk away from noise, from urgency, from distractions that pull you out of alignment.

It supports depth of impact. The space to give, to lead, to fund, to build without waiting for the next paycheck to tell you what is possible.

That is the power of becoming an architect. You stop living on someone else's schedule. You stop playing someone else's game. You stop following someone else's definition of success. And you begin designing around your own.

You are no longer limited to what you can earn in a year. You are building a system that works in the background. That system will not ask for permission. It will not take sick days. It will not burn out. It will keep working while you rest, while you think, while you create.

This is how freedom scales. Not in a rush. In design.

Start with what matters most. Your time. Your energy. Your relationships. Your values. Then build around them. Allocate to assets that reflect what you believe. Automate your process. Keep your strategy simple. Give your attention back to your life and let your capital do its job.

You are not just participating in the market. You are building something larger than yourself.

You are building a life that does not need to be escaped from.

A life where you own your mornings and your mindset.

A life where wealth supports purpose instead of distracting from it.

A life where your legacy is not just money left behind, but a model lived out in front of others.

From this point forward, you are no longer just an investor.

You are the architect of your freedom.

And your blueprint is already in motion.

CONCLUSION
THIS IS HOW FREEDOM IS BUILT

If you made it this far, then you are not just curious about wealth. You are ready to own it.

Not in theory. In action. Not someday. Right now.

This is the moment where information turns into transformation. Where a concept becomes a commitment. You have seen the math. You have studied the structure. You have absorbed the mindsets. And you now know something most people never understand.

Wealth is not mysterious. It is methodical.

It is not about luck. It is about alignment.

It is not about predicting. It is about positioning.

And the tools are right in front of you.

SMH and QQQ are not just tickers. They are access points to the future. They are how you align your capital with where the world is going. They represent the companies building the next chapter of the global economy. Platforms that scale. Semiconductors that power progress. Technology that moves civilization forward.

You are not investing in speculation. You are investing in infrastructure.

You are not just buying assets. You are buying time. Buying space. Buying back your life one contribution at a time.

And you now have the blueprint to turn that into a system.

You understand how to move beyond traditional advice that keeps you small.

You understand why innovation is the new land beneath our feet.

You understand how to automate discipline and protect your plan from noise.

You understand how to calculate what freedom really costs and what it really gives you.

You understand that wealth without clarity is just accumulation. But wealth with purpose is power.

You understand that the real threats are not market dips. They are hesitation, distraction, and misalignment.

And most importantly, you understand that the journey is not about chasing more.

It is about building enough.

Enough to choose. Enough to rest. Enough to lead with presence and give with intention. Enough to walk away from what no longer serves you and step fully into the life that does.

That is what this book was always about.

Not just financial literacy. Financial leadership.

Not just building portfolios. Building lives.

So here is what I leave you with.

Own your plan.

Own your process.

Own your timeline.

Own the assets that reflect the world you believe in.

Own the moments that test your conviction and strengthen it.

Own your definition of success and protect it from noise.

And most of all. Own the future.

Because no one else is going to do it for you.

And once you realize that you do not need permission, you will never wait again.

This is how freedom is built.

And this is where your ownership begins.

Printed in Dunstable, United Kingdom